W0112624

Writing Traditions

Revised Second Edition

Writing Programs Office
Department of English
Texas A&M University

Editorial assistants:
Amber Anderson • Laura Barker • Nicole DuPlessis • Matt Sherwood

KENDALL/HUNT PUBLISHING COMPANY
4050 Westmark Drive   Dubuque, Iowa 52002

Contents

Preface

In nearly every college in the United States, students are required to take a first-year English course in rhetoric and composition. Here you learn how to read and write persuasively in the academic world. You learn to handle the tasks of communication that people in every discipline must undertake—from engineering to education, from anthropology to agronomy. We have designed this book to help you do your best work in the rhetoric and composition course.

You should bring to the course a fair command of the basic elements of writing—the word, the sentence, the paragraph. Perhaps your work in high school also prepared you to write essays with clear theses and reports based on solid information. College English will allow you to extend your understanding and skill in the art of composing effective papers. Your writing will be based on readings from the great traditions of intellectual life and from the current stirrings of human thought and action. Your study and practice in this English course will smooth the way for your entrance into the various communities of learning that make up the modern university.

You will study such topics as the interplay of reading and writing; the relationship of thought and language; the writing process; the nature of authorship; the analysis of audiences, information, and contexts; effective organization, style, revision, and editing; use of the library; the best ways of selecting, evaluating, and documenting your sources; and techniques for reviewing your own work and that of other writers. During the semester, you will get extensive practice in writing and revising documented papers.

This guide will be the starting place for much of your work. Part I presents a general philosophy of rhetoric and composition and discusses what is involved in writing documented papers. Part II discusses resources for improving your writing. Part III offers worksheets to help you prepare papers and class assignments. Part IV provides a set of sample papers written by students in first year composition courses, and Part V covers University and English Department policies and procedures.

The sample papers in Part IV are not simple models for you to imitate. Nor are the practices recommended in Parts I and III simple formulas for good writing. Good writing is like any art or craft; it requires much practice and some experimentation. The aim of the composition course is to create a setting for your practice that is at once intellectually stimulating and practically effective. The aim of this book is to improve your understanding of your task and your performance in that writing environment.

Welcome to the world of academic writing.

Acknowledgments

Writing Traditions is truly a collaborative effort, the combined work of faculty, graduate assistant teachers, and undergraduate students who have allowed us to use their writing. This edition began with brainstorming, the exchange of ideas, and informal discussions—under the very capable leadership of Amber Anderson. The Writing Programs Office is most grateful to Amber for her contributions and also to Shane Trayers, Rebecca Caldwell, Cecilia Solis Sublette, and Lindsay Sloan for identifying student papers for this edition; to Kelli Perry for providing technical assistance; and to Nicole DuPlessis and Matt Sherwood for proofreading and editing the final manuscript.

This edition builds on the first edition (1998) of *Writing Traditions* edited by Susan Murphy and Margaret Strickland and published under the leadership of Valerie Balester. This edition also incorporates parts of two other previous Writing Programs Office publications: *Academic Writing*, by Joanna Barnett Gibson and M. Jimmie Killingsworth, and *A Guide to Writing at Texas A&M*, by Valerie Balester. Faculty and graduate assistant teachers who so generously contributed to these publications are listed below. Space does not allow for details of the role each person played, but each was significant.

FACULTY
Dr. M. Jimmie Killingsworth
Dr. Valerie Balester
Dr. Joanna Gibson

FORMER GRADUATE ASSISTANT TEACHERS:
Dr. Samuel L. Gladden
Dr. Jim Frost
Dr. Diana Ashe
Dr. Susan Murphy
Margaret Strickland
Thieu Brown

CURRENT GRADUATE ASSISTANT TEACHERS
Steve Marsden
Georgina Kennedy

Part I
Writing Skills

Introduction

Building a Strong Foundation

English 104, Composition and Rhetoric, is a foundation course—a prerequisite for other English courses and an introduction to college-level writing. It offers practice in many different kinds of writing assignments and encourages you to develop and refine skills you'll use throughout your academic career—especially critical thinking skills, critical reading skills, and effective writing skills. Major assignments in the course will require asking questions and considering multiple perspectives on a given topic; reading as a skeptic; understanding what kinds of information readers need and value; and shaping your own writing so that it meets your readers' needs and expectations.

Work in the classroom will vary. In addition to discussing strategies for improving your writing, you will participate in brainstorming sessions devoted to developing and narrowing writing topics; work in peer review sessions to review your classmates' drafts and offer suggestions for revision; and complete worksheets that ask you to reflect on your writing assignments or practice a specific skill, such as summarizing or paraphrasing another writer's work. During the semester, you should expect to write documented papers that require library research. You'll also submit in-class writing assignments that update your instructor on your progress with planning, drafting, revising, and editing an assignment. In other words, you will devote a good deal of your time this semester to working at the writer's trade: drafting and revising in order to communicate your thoughts and ideas clearly and effectively.

Writing Traditions introduces you to college-level writing. In addition to providing information about the course, this book offers exercises and worksheets that ask you to practice specific strategies: exploring ideas, narrowing topics, analyzing your intended readers, identifying appropriate sources, developing thesis statements, and understanding how to acknowledge other writers' words and ideas when you use them in your writing.

Practice, Practice, Practice

Like any other skill, writing requires practice. You enter the university with a good deal of experience as a writer, but you want to improve the skills you developed in high school or in a community college. You have to adjust to a new mindset now that you are part of the university academic community. English 104 asks you to write for your peers, your professors, and special interest groups on campus. These are diverse groups, rarely of one mindset, most often divided on current and enduring issues. As you draft papers, you'll need to consider more than one perspective; you have to investigate the most recent information on a topic, and you have to learn where to find sources that will be helpful to you and recognized as authoritative and reliable by your intended readers.

Major writing assignments include a series of short writing tasks intended to help you explore what you already know about a topic, what you want to know, and what you think your readers will find informative and interesting. Several of your assignments require library research; all of your assignments will require revision. You'll find yourself repeating a series of steps throughout the semester: planning, drafting, shaping, revising, and editing. These are the basic components of the writing process. With practice, you'll understand how to pace yourself when you have a major writing project or when you face writing under time constraints.

Creating a Writer's Workshop

Part of your task as a writer is identifying the locations that make you feel comfortable in your role as a writer and the tools that facilitate effective writing. When you draft and revise papers, you may have a preference for a quiet place in the library or you may favor one of the many computer labs on campus. Writers tolerate different levels of noise and interruption. You need to identify your comfort level with music, conversation, and other sounds on or off campus that can be distracting or inviting.

Research into the composing process reveals that the manner in which a writer begins a writing task and follows it through to the end is as personalized as a fingerprint. One person prefers drafting with a pencil and yellow legal pad; another person opts for drafting on a computer. The "tools of the trade" vary from writer to writer, too. Generally, writers need a dictionary, handbook, and thesaurus, pens and pencils, paper clips, erasers, and file folders. Calendars and planners can play an important role in the writing process, too.They allow writers to create individualized work schedules that help them meet due dates. The important point here is that you need to learn where you do your best writing and what you need to have at hand to plan, draft, revise, and edit your papers. You are the best judge of what it takes to create an environment that will facilitate your work as a student-writer.

Reading and Writing

Your experience as a writer has probably taught you that reading and writing are related skills. You usually can't excel as a writer if you neglect your role as a reader.You'll have opportunity to share drafts of your papers with your peers and to provide each other with constructive criticism. The final decisions about global revision and editing, though, are your own. You need to learn how to read your own writing with a critical eye, looking for ways to develop ideas fully, to articulate ideas clearly and coherently, to advance an argument in a logical manner, or to explain a complex concept in terms your readers will understand. Inexperienced writers very often produce a kind of egocentric writing— that is, writing that is aimed primarily at the writer, with little if any evidence of drafting and revising with other readers in mind. Learning to read your own writing with a critical eye is a strategy for avoiding egocentric writing. One of the goals of English 104 is for you to realize readers other than the instructor. You won't be writing for yourself and you won't be writing for the teacher. You should expect to write for many different kinds of readers.

Looking Ahead

As you adjust to the demands of college-level work, you'll find that courses across the disciplines require problem solving skills, critical reading skills, and effective writing skills. Good communication skills are one of the pathways to success in the academic and professional worlds. Take advantage of the opportunities you have this semester to hone those skills and to develop confidence as a writer.

Rhetoric and Composition

To begin your work in college writing, you need to have a reasonable command of English grammar and the mechanics of style (spelling, punctuation, capitalization, and so on). If you have trouble with these basic matters, you can use your handbook as a guide to improving your work, and you can get additional advice from your teacher and, if available on your campus, help from tutors in a writing center or writing lab.

Work in the classroom will focus on the development, organization, and presentation of information and ideas. The study of writing at this level usually involves the fields of *rhetoric* and *composition*.

What Is Rhetoric?

Rhetoric is the ancient art of developing and presenting information in an effective style. Defined as *the art of persuasion* in classical times, rhetoric is now considered more broadly as *the means by which authors communicate with their audiences by drawing upon shared knowledge and communal identities*.

When politicians, the most notorious of rhetorical speakers, appeal to an audience of farmers by suggesting that even Washington bureaucrats can have roots in farm life, they are trying to draw their listeners into an identification with them, so that the audience, persuaded of the speaker's understanding of their predicament and participation in their perspective, will accept the plan for action set forth in the speech. Or, when an advertisement waves an American flag, the aim is to appeal to the audience's patriotism so that, even if the ad is selling hot dogs, the product will be associated with the values of nationalism.

Beyond these well-known examples, we may discover more subtle uses of rhetoric. In academic life, where discourse is much more "objective," rhetoric still abounds. When philosophers or literary scholars place a thesis at the beginning of their essays to summarize their major arguments, they are, in addition to following the accepted conventions of writing in their fields, preparing their readers by providing a conceptual map for the rest of the paper; they are satisfying expectations in two ways—(1) by writing within a scheme known and accepted by the reader, and (2) by fulfilling the reader's need to see where the argument is leading. When sociologists summarize the recent trends of research in their field before they report and interpret their own research findings, they are (1) demonstrating their own command of key knowledge, (2) showing the reader that they are aware of the major problems in the field, and (3) proving the worth of their own work by asserting that it provides information that is new or different from what is already available. When scientists use a technical term like quark, or write sentences in the passive voice ("The measurement was taken") rather than the active voice ("I took the measurements"), or organize their papers in the IMRaD format (Introduction, Methods, Results, and Discussion), they are also appealing to a community of writers and readers who share their own outlook toward the world and their own way of describing that world and giving value to it.

In short, rhetoric plays a vital role not only in writing but also in the creation of new knowledge in all academic fields. All writing that shows an awareness of audience is rhetorical.

The Elements of Rhetoric

Rhetoric involves five major elements:

- the *author*, or the perspective from which the information is delivered, the point of view represented by the *I* or *we* of the paper (even when use of the first-person pronouns is avoided);
- the *audience*, or the *you* of the paper, the perspective to which appeals are addressed, usually with the hope that some shift in perspective will occur;

- the *subject matter*, or information contained in the paper;
- the *text*, the written or spoken medium, the language of the paper; and
- the *context*, the social and historical background of the author and the audience.

The galvanizing principle that pulls all of these elements together into a forceful communication is **purpose**. In evaluating your rhetorical situation, you should ask, Why am I writing? What is my objective? What do I expect my readers to do after they read my paper? Will I change the way they think or act? (If I don't, why should I bother to write?) What information do the readers need before they can think or act according to the new perspective I give them? What styles and kinds of writing should I use to make the information most accessible to them?

We study rhetoric in order to write better papers. The claim of rhetorical study is that, by increasing your understanding of the five elements and by analyzing your purpose, you will increase your chances of producing a good paper. A systematic application of rhetorical analysis will also improve your reading. You will learn to approach texts carefully and critically— both your own texts and those of other writers.

Composition—The Writing Process

Composition is the *application of rhetoric to the writing process*. Whenever you write, you work through a definite set of stages or steps. These vary from writer to writer, but they usually involve a definite set of tasks:

- planning—everything you do to prepare for writing, from gathering information to talking to your teachers and colleagues to making outlines or notes,
- drafting—the act of transforming a blank page or computer screen into a written text,
- revision—the act of reviewing your paper (becoming your own reader) and rewriting to improve its thoroughness and effectiveness,
- editing—the process of putting on the finishing touches, fine-tuning your sentences, and cleaning up errors,
- production—the final preparation of the paper on a word processor or typewriter.

We urge you to take a rhetorical view of composition, treating each stage of the process as an opportunity to examine your perspective and subject matter, to hone your ideas and question your information. In planning, you should construct in your mind a realistic picture of the rhetorical situation. In drafting, you should push your writing toward thorough coverage of your topic, paying attention to your feelings about the adequacy of each sentence and paragraph, but reserving attention to the finer points of style and language use till later. In revising, you should strive to see the paper as your reader will. In editing, you should aim for the style that will be most appealing and readable for your audience. And, in typing, you should create a neat, attractive, and professional document, a document that will be pleasing and easy to read.

The process rarely goes forward in this nice linear manner. Most students, like most professional writers, now prefer to type papers onto a word processor as early as possible. That way, revision and correction don't have to wait until the whole paper is done. You can start writing the paper in the middle and then go back and write the introduction. At that point, you'll know exactly where the paper is going, and you can thus serve as a better guide for your reader.

If you develop a flexible version of the writing process, you will increase your chances of getting the best information in the best place and presenting it in the best way. And that's what composition is all about.

What Other Courses Provide a Background in Composition and Rhetoric?

The Department of English offers the following courses that focus on Composition and Rhetoric.

English 210	Technical Writing
English 241	Advanced Composition
English 301	Technical Writing
English 310	History of the English Language
English 320	Technical Editing and Writing
English 353	History of Rhetoric
English 354	Modern Rhetorical Theory
English 355	Rhetoric of Style
English 461	Advanced Syntax and Rhetoric

The Department of English offers English majors the opportunity to explore literature, creative writing, and rhetoric. For information about an English major or minor, contact the English Department Undergraduate Office in Blocker 223.

Academic Research and Writing

In every discipline within an academic organization, what counts as information will change. Research is the development of information according to an agenda and a methodology established by the history and current inclinations of each special community of discourse. Humanists study texts in the library. Scientists, social scientists, and engineers build models, do experiments, and make designs.

But every discipline has its literature, a set of texts that the members of the profession consider exemplary and important. Reviewing this literature is a component of all significant work in academic life, and that is why in freshman English we teach you to discover, study, reveal, and shape information from sources in the library. Since English teachers have been trained in the humanistic tradition and since they have a special interest in language and in the act of forging new discourse out of existing discourses, they are particularly well prepared to guide you in this kind of work.

The aim of research in the library is not to compile mounds of disconnected facts, but to shape information into knowledge, to give it a structure and a meaning that may not be obvious at first glance. Reviews of the literature in any field are directed by a good topic—a theme that gives meaning and structure to the search for data as well as to the presentation of data. A topic is first of all a principle for selecting which information you will consider in your writing. If your topic is "Effects of Global Warming on the Environmental Movement," for example, you will probably not read articles on acid rain, unless you discover that global warming and acid rain are connected in a special way. You will instead focus your research on the key words of your topic—*global warming* and *environmental movement*—either of which you could use in searching indexes and databases in the library.

You will need to talk closely with your professors and colleagues about what counts as good information and what kinds of topics are important in your field. You will also need to read critically and analytically, to get at the meaning and purpose of other people's writing.

What Discipline Does Your Major Fall Under?

HUMANITIES	SOCIAL SCIENCES	HARD SCIENCES
English	Psychology	Biology
Philosophy	Sociology	Botany
Theatre, Dance & Film	Political Science	Chemistry
Languages	Education	Zoology
Economics	Government	Physics
Anthropology	Public Service	Mathematics
American Studies	School Psychology	Applied Mathematics

Selecting Appropriate Sources

College Level Research

One of your goals in college courses should be to examine what the academic community has said about a given topic. Books published by university presses and articles published in academic journals usually provide the most reliable information and, for articles in journals, the most recently published information on the topic. Encyclopedias are no longer a source, but perhaps just used for background information.

Scholarly Sources

These sources are usually written by experts to one of two audiences, experienced (other experts) and inexperienced (audience with a college education). Either way they are targeting the academic community. These books or articles are usually peer-reviewed, meaning that they have been read and evaluated by other experts in that area. They follow a formal style of documentation —such as MLA or APA—which will include footnotes, endnotes, or citations with a works cited page.

Popular Sources

These sources are usually something you can buy in a store or access online. The audience is usually a more general and public audience with a layperson's knowledge, as opposed to an academic one. These sources are often affiliated with the news and do not usually have a lot of analysis. It is important to consider your audience and rhetorical situation when using popular sources; you have a much different role when writing for a popular source than you do when you write for a scholarly source.

Internet Sources

Some scholarly journals, newspapers, and magazines publish electronic versions on the Internet. The Internet also contains other Web sites that may or may not provide reliable information on the topic. These sites include government, business, organization, university, and individual homepages. The Internet can be a source for locating up-to-date information and further references; however, anyone can publish anything on the Web, accurate or not. Always verify any information obtained off the Internet; it must be viewed with some skepticism. Before beginning research, check with your instructor to learn his or her policies regarding Internet sources.

What's Available on the Internet?

The information highway can be a source for scholarly research, but it is crucial to evaluate any kind of electronic source. The endings on the web addresses can be a clue to who has published a Web site:

- **.com:** company Web site. You will find these most of the time.
- **.org:** organization, usually non-profit.
- **.edu:** educational institution (university, college, etc.) site.
- **.mil:** military site
- **.gov:** government site.

Library
Resources

Evans Library

The Sterling C. Evans library, located in the middle of the main campus, across from the History Building, is the general academic library on the Texas A&M campus. It houses books, periodicals, maps, audio-visual materials, special collections, and government documents and offers students areas for individual and group study. You should expect to use the resources in this library for English 104 assignments. If your instructor does not schedule a tour for your class, you can attend a library tour on your own at the beginning of the semester. Check the general reference desk on the first floor of the Evans Library for a schedule. These tours will introduce you to services provided by the Evans Library.

Annex

Located across from Evans, the Annex is adjacent to the Pavilion. It houses computer labs, study rooms, microforms, reserves, and Educational Media Services. A virtual tour of the annex is available online.

Electronic Resources

LibCat is the University Libraries' online catalog system. You will use it to look up call numbers for books, journals, and other documents. The Texas A&M Library System also provides access to databases and electronic journals. Several of the databases are listed below to give you an idea of the scope of the resources available to you through the Evans Library.

Electronic Abstracts, Indexes and Databases

- Access UN   access through: http://library.tamu.edu/ resources/

- CIAO   http://www.ciaonet.org/

- EconLit-Cambridge Scientific Abstracts access through: http://library.tamu.edu/ resources/

- Global Newsbank   access through: http://library.tamu.edu/ resources/

- GPO Access   http://www.access.gpo.go v/su_docs/index.html

- Lexis-Nexis: Academic Universe, Congressional Universe, Statistical Universe, and Government Periodicals Universe   access through: http://library.tamu.edu/ resources/

- Political Science Abstracts   access through: http://library.tamu.edu/ resources/

- Tex Share Newspapers (Infotrac)   access through: http://library.tamu.edu/ resources/

- Web of Science   http://www.webofscience. com/

In addition to the Evans Library on the main campus, TAMU students have access to other library facilities that are part of the Texas A&M Library System. For directions and guidelines on using these resources, see the Texas A&M Libraries' Web page.

Cushing Memorial Library

Located behind Evans Library, the Cushing Memorial Library includes a variety of resources—for example, rare books, maps, pamphlets, manuscripts, photographs, newspapers, government documents, microfilm, audiotapes, videotapes, and many other materials, including special collections. Because of the specialized nature of some of these materials, the Library recommends that you contact them in advance if you want to use special collections.

West Campus Library

Located next to the Wehner building, the West Campus Library includes books and other resources used by students and faculty in Business, Agriculture and Life Science, Animal Science, Biochemistry, Biophysics, Entomology, Forest Science, Horticulture, Poultry Science, and Soil and Crop Sciences.

Policy Sciences and Economics Library (PSEL)

Providing library services for political science and economics, PSEL is located on the first floor of the George Bush School of Government and Public Service, which is in the Academic Building West. PSEL houses books, current periodicals, electronic resources, and special collections.

The Medical Sciences Library

Located on West campus, the Medical Sciences Library serves the Health Science Center and the College of Veterinary Medicine.

The George Bush Presidential Library

One of ten presidential libraries in the nation, the George Bush Library holds official records and personal papers of our forty-first President. Administered by the National Archives and Records Administration, this library is located on the west campus. If you plan to do research here, you should write, call, or e-mail the Bush Library staff in advance of any visit to find out if the library has material that will be useful in your research project.

Analyzing Academic Writing

Rhetoric provides a way of analyzing writing that will help you to read critically and analytically. You will need to read as a writer, always taking in information that will be useful to you as you develop your own research.

Your biggest question will always be this: How does the purpose of the text you are reading coincide with your own purpose for writing and the purpose of the community's research program? Along the way to answering this question, you will also consider the other rhetorical elements of the writing under review:

- the *author:* What is the perspective from which the information is delivered, the point of view represented by the *I* or *we* of the paper? With which community of discourse or discipline of study does the author seem to identify? Is the author an expert on the topic or rather a reporter of other expert views of the information? Does the author want to change the way you think or the way you act? How? What is the author's attitude toward the information and audience of the paper (tone)?

- the *audience*: Who is the *you* of the text, the perspective to which the information is addressed? How is the information shaped to appeal to that audience? How is the reader expected to respond to the information—with surprise, concern, action? Is the reader a member of the same community of discourse represented by the author?

- the *subject matter*: What information is new and different to you? How is it different from information contained in other texts you have encountered in your research? How is it structured or organized? What seems to receive the most emphasis?

- the *text*: Is the language of the text unusual or striking, or would you consider it typical of writing in the author's community? Does the language change as the text covers different parts of the information?

- the *context*: What is the social and historical background of the author and the audience, the time and place, the scene of the presentation of this information? How could the context have affected the author's emphasis or judgments about the information?

COMMUNICATION TRIANGLE

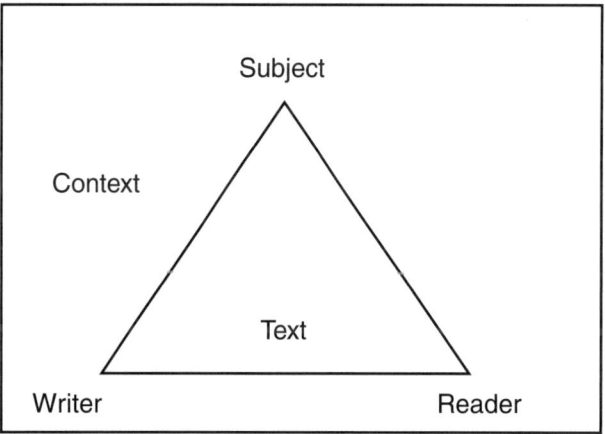

Kinds
of Assignments

Academic writing varies greatly from field to field, as you will discover in this course and in your student career as a whole. The best we can do in a course on general writing is to help you learn how to develop papers organized on a few basic models and then teach you to ask questions about special forms of discourse.

Formal Papers

Formal writing is for someone other than yourself. Readers have expectations that writers have to satisfy. Your first step in getting used to giving readers what they need is learning to follow assignments for writing that affect form as well as content. Listen to your teacher carefully and ask questions when the assignment for a formal paper is made.

The papers in your first-year English course will use a variety of structural patterns. These may include the following:

1. **The narrative essay**. A *narrative* tells a story. An *essay* provides a commentary organized around a thesis, or main idea. In a *narrative essay*, you give an account of an event, which you have read about in your textbook or in a news source; then you comment on the significance of that event. *Example:* You write a paper that tells about the recent fires in the Rocky Mountains and comments on the significance of this event for the people and animals of Colorado.

2. **The expository essay**. This paper focuses on the thesis as a means of making sense of a body of information for the reader. The reader's understanding of the information and outlook on the world should be changed after reading the essay. Narrative still plays a role in your framing of examples to illustrate your thesis. These illustrative examples are condensed narratives of significant events. *Example:* You write a paper that shows how large-scale, low-technology industries pose an increasing threat to the natural environment. You illustrate your point with references to giant oil spills, the problem of toxic waste, and the threat of acid rain and global climate change.

3. **The review of literature.** Just as every culture has a literature, or at least a cherished set of stories and myths, every academic field has a literature, a body of texts that contains the most highly valued information in the field. A literature review is a kind of expository essay. It comments upon what the available literature has to say about a specific topic or problem. *Example:* You report on recent findings in the field of atmospheric chemistry about the current state of the ozone layer. You should not merely go through and summarize your sources one at a time, but you should organize the information you find according to reasonable divisions of the topic. The sections of your paper may answer a series of questions, with information derived from your sources presented in the appropriate places: What is the ozone layer? Why is it important? What is the evidence for damage to the ozone? What further research is needed?

4. **The argumentative essay**. This paper may have the form of a narrative or an expository essay, but the aim is different. Rather than just increasing the information available to the reader or changing the way the reader thinks about the information, you may actually want to change the way the reader acts. *Example:* You write a paper on industrial damage to the environment that argues for a shift to smaller-scale, de-centralized, hightech industry. Or, going to the other side, you defend the overall environmental record of heavy industry, arguing that the benefits outweigh the costs.

5. **Delayed thesis essay**. This essay does not form its argument until the very end. Instead of arguing a viewpoint throughout this essay, the author instead presents two opposing viewpoints about a topic.

Both sides are presented fairly, equally, and without bias. The author also presents the points the perspectives have in common. The paper may conclude with a favorable response to one perspective, or it may develop a new argumentative stance that is somewhere in the middle of the two perspectives under review. Because this essay is a type of argument by negotiation, both sides need to feel they have been heard and presented positively, thoroughly, and fairly. With this kind of overview, readers are likely to accept whatever comments you present at the end of the paper.

6. **Rhetorical analysis essay**. This paper takes a *close reading* of a published author's stance on an issue and the argument the author develops to advance and support that stance. While the paper provides a brief summary of the article, the primary goal is to *analyze* what makes it effective, mediocre, or ineffective. Points to consider include, but are not limited to, how the author addresses intended readers; uses tone, evidence, data, and any material fallacies; and appeals to logic, emotion, or authority. In addition to evaluating how the author meets his or her aim in writing, this paper explains whether you agree or disagree with the author's stance on any particular issue.

7. **Conversion of one type of writing into another**. This project calls for global revision—a complete reworking at all levels—of a paper written earlier in the course. You will incorporate at least one additional source, as well as headings in the text, and either a table or figure in the text. You'll write for a new audience, too. When a writer takes something she's already written and makes it appropriate for a different rhetorical situation, the writer has to consider the needs of the new audience, the needs of the genre that she will be rewriting in, and the needs of the message that she wishes to convey. *Example:* A writer has completed an informative, documented academic paper about the science of genetically-modified foods (GMF). She decides to draft an editorial about the safety of GMF use. To convert her original document to another genre and another rhetorical situation, she selects appropriate scientific data that establishes her point briefly and clearly, as she will be limited in the number of words to express her opinion. She will also reorganize the chosen data around her primary persuasive argument. Finally, she will need to reformat her document into an appropriate newspaper-editorial style and change her documentation style to fit journalism standards.

Informal Writing

Informal writing is less conscious of a critical audience than is formal writing. Your course will present occasions for informal writing, for example Web journals or reader-response papers, in which you can let down your guard and have a written conversation with your teacher, your peers, or yourself. You don't want to let down your guard too much, though. A word of caution here: *Don't get overly personal or intimate in informal writing assignments.* Think of any writing assignment for the course as a public record of your private thoughts, a piece of writing that, though informal, is still an open book. Anything you write for a course assignment should be appropriate for sharing with the class as a whole.

Narrowing Your Topic

Coming up with a topic can be one of the most challenging parts of writing a paper. If you are told to "find a topic" and you have not had experience selecting or narrowing a topic on your own, a panicky writer's block may strike. But you can and will overcome it with practice and diligence. Your strategy should be first to select a topic that interests you, one that seems appropriate for the assignment and the group of intended readers you've selected (or been assigned). Examples will follow that illustrate how writers move from broad general topics to sufficiently narrowed topics that give focus to research and writing.

Don't be surprised if your instructor restricts you from writing about certain topics. Consider any restrictions friendly advice—it is intended to help you avoid topics that are rarely successful in short papers or are impossible to prove in the best of circumstances. Accept your instructor's expertise on this matter, and think again.

You may be surprised by your instructor telling you that "gun control" or "abortion" or "the death penalty" are not topics. Indeed, these are issues, but you must narrow to a very specific aspect of one of these issues before you have a topic for a writing assignment. For instance, "the death penalty" is not a topic, but if you narrow to a discussion of how the death penalty affects people, it is still much too broad, but it is on its way to being an acceptable topic. If you narrow to choose a specific group of people (general public, citizenry of the state that performed the execution, other criminals in the state, the community the person executed came from, family of the person executed, family of the victim of the person executed), you can narrow your topic again. For example, you might choose to discuss the effects of execution on the families of the victim of the person executed. You still have a large body of people to research and not much space in your paper; perhaps, you narrow the topic to family who watched the execu-

tion—and you might need to narrow regional, economic, and religious factors.

Now, you have a much more specific issue, but you have not yet chosen a side or determined what criteria you will use to judge the effects of execution on the victim's family. Let's say you decide to study the effects of the execution on activities outside the home, work performance, and amount of time the family spends together. Library research will help you determine the way to focus an issue.

By having a narrowed topic, you can streamline research and avoid broad, general discussions. This is why your instructor will caution you against picking a topic that is too general and unfocused. With a narrowed topic, you'll find that works cited and bibliographies in one source frequently lead you to other important information. For example, a journal article on the effects of execution on victims' families might cite a source that includes interviews with family and their co-workers.

Don't limit yourself by thinking that the only appropriate topic for a persuasive or argumentative paper is a nationally controversial topic. There are many local issues that lend themselves to successful coverage in a 3-10 page paper much better than the big hot topics. An issue that you know from your hometown (should your town zone to restrict superstores from coming in and hurting local business?), your community (are there inappropriate advertisements near elementary schools?), your school (how should your school raise extra funds to create a program you wish to see established?), or even your work (are casual dress requirements helping or hurting employee productivity?) may be much more interesting reading and more feasible research than a major controversy that has no new arguments to add to the discussion.

So, remember, pick a topic and narrow according to:

the type of research you have access to: the appropriate research must be present in your paper to be successful; a lack of access to research is not an excuse for a vague, unsupported paper, it is your responsibility to pick a topic that you can successfully research.

an appropriate scope: a paper with a broad scope usually ends up relying on generalizations and discussions that are vague and undefined. An essay that takes this kind of approach will not be successful. With a narrowed scope, however, you should have a good sense of the type of research you need to support your arguments. You can set up the criteria you intend to follow as you argue, making sure that you have support for those criteria. Whether your assignment requires that you use two or three sources to prove your point or ten or twelve sources to support a broader argument, a topic narrowed in scope will give focus to library research.

an appropriate audience: often, your audience is chosen for you, so you might think that it is fixed and not an issue that you need to consider. However, you are responsible for making sure that your paper is convincing, relevant, and interesting to the audience (whether you have chosen it or have had it assigned). One of the best guidelines to follow is to avoid the obvious—topics and arguments readers have heard or seen repeatedly in the news. If you really want to write about a topic that has received heavy media attention, try to take a stance that has a fresh perspective.

your purpose: why are you writing this paper in the first place? Are you evaluating, informing, persuading, negotiating, or entertaining? Whatever your purpose, it is important to understand both what your audience already understands and what you want them to understand by the end of the essay. If you are discussing an issue familiar to your audience and you know that the audience agrees with you, it is important to present new reasons for their continued support. Rehashing what they already know would only bore them. If you discuss an issue that is unfamiliar to them, you should present the foundation of the issue clearly, even if you think it goes without saying. Most important, you should make sure that the audience follows your argument easily from what they already know about your topic through to what you want them to know about your topic. Whatever the genre you are writing in, this is the purpose of writing: to have an audience (friendly or antagonistic) understand why you have come to believe what you believe and why you wish for them to understand or even to act according to your beliefs.

Let's look at another example of narrowing a topic—inappropriate ads near an elementary school. Our audience will be citizens of our hometown. It might be good to consider who makes up that audience: how large is the population? what are the percentages of races? how many religions are represented? how does the community typically vote in an election? how many newspapers are there? what types of stories most often make up the first two pages of the local newspaper?

Let's say our hometown has a large and diverse population of over 500,000. The city's population statistics show 43% white, 22% African-American, 15% Hispanic, 6% Asian, and 14% other, which includes but is not limited to Native Americans, Arabic peoples, and Indians. This community also has a large university, and so the population is educated above the national average. You look in the phone book, under churches and see Catholic and Protestant churches, synagogues, Buddhist and Hindu temples, and Islamic mosques. The community has had five Democratic mayors, three Republican mayors, and two Independent mayors in the last ten elections, so it seems to be a moderately liberal community in its politics. There is one local newspaper, and it often runs national events, special interest, highly-individualized articles, and international news in the first two pages.

Seeing this, you decide to focus on religious advertisements near elementary schools. You have noticed that there are signs that advocate principles from a certain religion that are within sight of an elementary school playground. The sign changes every month and has become a focal point for conversation with the children, leading them to ask their teachers to explain the signs and give their opinion about them.

The teachers are not sure how to respond, as they are typically not allowed to address religious issues in school. You decide, whether you agree with the messages on the signs or not, that the signs are causing too big of a problem for the public school teachers of a diverse religious population.

You decide to discuss the legality of the placement of those signs. You write an informative and persuasive essay to an audience of your hometown city council that aims to persuade the city to remove signs of a religious nature from the proximity of an elementary school.

You begin to think of sources and call the elementary school in question to get an interview with one of the teachers who has faced difficult questions and can explain her inability to address those questions in a public school forum. You go to the library to ask a librarian for aid in finding a scholarly source that explains the legal precedent for the separation of church and state, as it has been most recently interpreted. The librarian helps you with a legal database like *Lexus-Nexus*. You also decide to look for articles about the restriction of tobacco ads from the proximity of public schools. You now know that you have a topic that has something to argue and has research to support it; narrowing is complete, and reading and drafting may begin.

As this example illustrates, the most important guideline to follow for topic selection is to choose a topic that interests you personally and to narrow it sufficiently. By narrowing the scope of broad, general topics, you give focus to library research and you have a good chance of developing a paper that is interesting and relevant to your intended readers.

Part II
Constructive Criticism

Developing Your Perspective

As an author, you always write from a certain **perspective** or **stance**, representing either a personal viewpoint, a special body of knowledge, or a social group. The way you handle your perspective helps to convey the **tone** of the communication—your attitude toward the audience and subject matter of the writing. Your tone is a result of your word choice, sentence structure, and use of persuasive techniques.

Say, for example, that you are a nuclear physicist presenting a report on the safety of a reactor to a local town council. You will speak from the perspective of an *expert* representing the most capable knowledge in the field of nuclear physics. If you speak *only* from the expert perspective, however, as if you were speaking to a group of fellow physicists, your audience will feel left out or overwhelmed. So you must also think and talk from the perspective of a responsible citizen and convey a tone of *helpfulness*. If you tone down your subject too much, however, you may appear to be condescending to the audience, treating them like children. So your perspective must also be tempered by *respect*. You will then present your information in a way appropriate for a nonexpert but educated audience. Your perspective is that of a helpful and respectful expert.

If you are used to writing your papers mainly for an audience of teachers, you may feel that your perspective is limited by the need to prove that you know the material nearly as well as the teacher or at least as well as your classmates. This outlook often leads to showy writing that is concerned more with impressing the audience than with communicating information. Such showiness may be defensive, an effort to cover up for what you perceive to be a deficiency in knowledge.

Remember, even if your audience knows more about your topic than you do, you still have something to offer. Since every person has a unique set of experiences, every writer potentially has something new to bring to old subject matter. You can create a surprise for your teacher by offering a new interpretive twist on your topic or by bringing knowledge from other fields to bear on the subject matter of your paper. There have been, for example, medical interpretations of *The Scarlet Letter* and philosophical analyses of Darwin's theory of evolution.

If you are writing for your classmates, you should select and develop topics that allow you to bring them new information presented in a new way.

The Undergraduate University Writing Center

The Undergraduate University Writing Center is a place for all writers, from beginners to experienced. It provides Texas A&M University students with one-on-one writing assistance. The Writing Center's consultants will help you with any stage of writing: rough drafts, grammar, organization, citation, or revision. Their goal is to help you improve your writing and to give you the skills and confidence to work independently. Although the Writing Center does not proofread, consultants can help you identify strengths and weaknesses in your work, and teach you to improve your proofreading skills.

Services and Goals

- The Writing Center offers handouts on just about every aspect of writing. You may obtain these by printing copies off their Web page, or you may go to the Writing Center and pick them up.
- You may also sign up for a session with a consultant. All consultants are writers themselves and have taught, tutored, or worked as professional writers.

Location and Contact Information

- Location: **Evans Library** on the second floor, room 210.B.
- Phone Number: **(979) 458–1455**.
- Web address: **http://uwc.tamu.edu.**

You may use any of these to contact the Writing Center for help or to set up an appointment.

Appointments

- Each session lasts 30–45 minutes and begins on the hour.

- Drop-ins are welcome. If someone is more than five minutes late for an appointment, that person forfeits the appointment time. Since consultants are usually very busy when papers are due, you should make an appointment at least 24 hours in advance.

What to Expect

- Sessions are most productive when you bring a copy of your assignment, and when you come to the session aware of what you'd like to work on. The more specific you can be, the better the consultant will be able to help you.
- If you have a paper in written form when you visit the Writing Center, you may sit down with a tutor and read it aloud. The two of you will discuss the areas of the document that you wish to focus on. If you have not written the paper, the consultant will discuss it with you and help you get started.
- Writing Center policies prevent consultants from discussing your instructor, his or her comments, or your grades.
- The Writing Center does not proofread papers, and your consultants are not responsible for pointing out every flaw they see for you to correct. In other words, they are not editors. Their goal is to help you critique and edit your own writing. Your session will be directed by your greatest concerns, so for the best outcome, you'll need to do some work before your visit. Writing Center consultants are useful resources. They will work with you one on one to help you gain confidence in the revising and critiquing of your own work.

Making the Best of a Student-Teacher Conference

One of the quickest, easiest and best ways to improve your writing is to talk with your writing instructor at all stages in your writing process, especially at the drafting and revising stages. In fact, most English 104 instructors designate several classroom sessions as conference hours, times when students meet with instructors on an individual basis to discuss such things as the writing process, brainstorming, rough drafts, revision strategies, and specific writing challenges. When teacher-student conferences have been productive and successful, they help student writers become aware of audience concerns and adept at solving their own writing problems. Effective teacher-student conferences also remind students that talking with others—something we do all the time—is one of the most powerful learning tools available. During your conference, try the following techniques to make it most productive:

- **Relax**. Although you may be intimidated by the thought of one-on-one conversation with your writing instructor, remember that your instructor wants to help you explore what you've done well on a particular piece of writing as well as what you both think needs improvement.
- **Come Prepared**. Come to the conference with a clear task in mind, whether it's brainstorming, working on a thesis statement, or getting a reader's response to the examples you've used in a particular paper. Even if the instructor has designated a topic for the conference—talking about research proposals, for example—arrive ready to talk about your ideas.
- **Reflect**. In a journal or in an e-mail to your instructor, summarize what you gained from your conference. This kind of reflection serves as a record of your visit, but more importantly, it is a reminder to you and your instructor of the conversation that took place, the ideas you shared, and the questions you asked.
- **Talk**. Ask questions; there are no stupid questions. Listen to your instructor; repeat what the instructor tells you to make sure you heard him or her correctly.
- **Don't be afraid to admit you don't understand something your instructor has said**. If you don't understand something your instructor says, let your instructor know that you are trying to follow the conversation, but you still need help. For example, if you visited the office to discuss a paper, you might say something like this: "I understand that you want me to include more proofs in my paper, but I don't understand what you mean by proofs. Can you give me an example?" Typically, instructors respond to this kind of question by offering an example and then directing students to additional explanations in their textbooks. The point to be made here is really very simple: If you don't understand something, ask for help. Whether you are asking about papers, grades, or homework assignments, be diplomatic, be patient, and be attentive.
- **Take notes**. It is not rude to write while someone is talking. Feel free to ask your instructor to repeat something that seems particularly useful, so that you may write it down accurately. You may not remember everything you discuss with your instructor by the time you are working on your paper again. Good notes can make all the difference.

Peer Critiques

During the semester, you'll work in groups to review drafts of papers before you submit them for evaluation. The more preparation you put into a peer review draft, the more feedback you should expect from your classmates. The directions that follow serve as guidelines on preparing peer review drafts.

Peer Review Drafts

To allow for *your* annotations as well as comments from your peers, double space and increase your right- and left-hand margins from 1" to 2". Your peer review drafts should include your annotations identifying passages in your paper you consider effective or ineffective or places where you really need feedback. With these wide margins, the text will be much longer than the draft you submit for grading. Here's an example:

Impostor in Texas? The Mystery of Blanche Sweet

In September 1992, fifteen years after his death, Elvis showed up on the outskirts of Corsicana, Texas, prepared to "hound and dog Bill Clinton's bus tour of the state" by passing out baloney sandwiches as "commentary" on the Clinton campaign ("King" 148). The King's "shenanigans … [ended] in an Athens, Texas, Dairy Queen where … [he] lapped up ice cream while signing autographs" ("King" 148). *People Weekly* reported that the Republican Elvis bore an amazing resemblance to Victor Solimine, 42, a government employee living in Pflugerville, Texas. As a government employee, Mr. Solimine was prohibited by the Hatch Act from campaigning for candidates; so, understandably, he denied any role in the political hyjinks and insisted the Republican Elvis must have been the real thing ("King" 148).

Is the title appropriate?

Does the introduction create interest in the topic?

Should I spell this? Is the number ok?

Do I need to explain what this is?

I'm delaying my thesis on purpose. Does the introduction seem too long? Should I revise and state the thesis early in the papers?

The press coverage this incident generated illustrates a universal fascination with Elvis sightings, political one-ups-manship, and, most importantly, authenticity. The incident is one of the few documented reports in Texas of an individual passing himself off as a celebrity—and, in this case, *you* might reasonably assume, the citizens of Corisicana and Athens were participants in the fun rather than suckers duped by a con artist. You might also assume that Texas has played host to its share of impostors because so many of our communities are ideal targets-remote, separated from the more densely populated areas of the state by distance and loneliness, populated with people eager to rub elbows with celebrities, people who would, perhaps, readily make themselves willing victims.

In another documented case of an impostor in Texas, however, the target community was Houston. In 1979, a reporter from *The Houston Post* learned that Patricia Wallenda, who claimed to be granddaughter of the famous Karl Wallenda had been transferred to Sam Houston Memorial Hospital after falling earlier in the week from a forty-foot high wire during a performance in Boston (Flood A 13). The transfer accommodated Ms. Wallenda's wish to see a relative and to…

Should I say "you" or "one?" "One" seems very formal.

I'm trying to provide lots of examples of impostors in Texas to show that there is clearly a problem. Do I have enough examples? Too many?

Does this claim seem too general? Do I need documentation?

Do I need to explain why he was famous?

Document Design

Document design is the integration of text and visual design to facilitate a better understanding of a document for the reader. A well-designed document should effectively meet the needs of the reader. Also, the visual structure of a document should be consistent throughout the document. Three important aspects of document design are:

- typography
- spatial cueing or white space
- color

Start planning the visual design of your document before you actually begin writing the document itself. Visual design should not be an afterthought to "dress up" a document, but rather an important planning stage where you incorporate visual features to help delineate the meaning or purpose of the document to the reader.

Typography

Typography, or type, is one of the basic design elements of a document. It affects the overall readability and effectiveness of the document. With so many options available on computers, you may be overwhelmed at the number of typefaces to choose from. You should use a typeface that is readable and works well with the document, not one that is merely aesthetically pleasing. Selecting typeface is a practical choice, not an artistic one.

Perhaps the easiest decision when choosing typeface for a document is whether to use a serif or sans serif font.

Serif fonts have up and down strokes that help blend letters together horizontally. Serif fonts bind letters into groups making them effective for large chunks of text.

Sans Serif fonts do not have serifs. Sans serif fonts have a crisper and cleaner appearance and are more effective as headers or in posters and advertisements.

There are many other typographical choices you can make besides choosing between a serif and sans serif font that can cue the reader's attention. Changing the typeface, size, and weight of a type can give the reader a cue as to what is contained in the text.

There are many different categories of typefaces, and each is effective when used appropriately. Remember, you should use a typeface that is appropriate for the document.

Grettin is a decorative font for the appearance of calligraphy.

Zapf Chancery is an ornate script font with a formal appearance.

`Courier` is a classic font with a "typewriter" appearance.

Kidprint is a crazy font for a fun appearance.

Italicizing text helps draw attention and highlight information for the reader. Italicizing is a good way to show emphasis.

abcdefghijklmnopqrstuvwxyz   Roman
abcdefghijklmnopqrstuvwxyz   *Italic*

Changing the size of the type is another way to highlight and distinguish the type for the reader. For collegiate writing, the standard size is either 10, 11, or 12 point. These sizes are considered text type. Anything over 12 point is considered display type and can be used to cue the reader or for advertising. Larger fonts are effective for headings. Changing the size of the headings gives them a hierarchy (i.e., the largest font would be a main heading and anything smaller would be a subheading).

A   A   A   A   A   A   A   A   A   A   A

10 pt.   12pt.   14pt.   16pt.   18pt.   20pt.   22pt.   24pt.   26pt.   28pt.   30pt.

Another way to draw attention to the text is to boldface it. Like italicizing, boldface text effectively emphasizes information. Also, combining variations in text size with boldface helps distinguish heading hierarchy.

ABCDEFGHIJKLMNOPQRSTUVWXYZ
Regular
ABCDEFGHIJKLMNOPQRSTUVWXYZ
Boldface

It is important to understand that the variations of text must be apparent to the reader for them to be effective cues. Do not overdo it. If you boldface or italicize too often, then you will lose the meaning of the distinction. Also avoid capitalizing all the letters, because it makes the text hard to read. Understand that the purpose of cueing is to make the document easier for the reader to use.

Typographical cueing is an effective way to highlight information for the reader, but it is most effective with the help of spatial cueing, or the use of white space.

Spatial Cueing

Spatial cueing is the use of white or blank space to frame or emphasize the text. White space frames the text and makes the information more accessible and easier to read. The easiest way to organize information is to chunk the text into manageable blocks. Chunking information divides the text by separation and isolates the information as well. Below, Figure 1 shows a document that is in a large block of text and Figure 2 shows a document that is chunked using spatial changes.

Another effective way to chunk information is to combine typographical cueing with spatial changes.

This way, the information is not only highlighted by spatial differences, but the change in type (i.e., boldface and make the size of font larger) also cues the reader. Figure 3 is an example of a document that is chunked both spatially and typographically.

Typographical and spatial cueing are complimentary. They are most effective when used together. You should not substitute one for the other. For instance, you decide to distinguish headings from text by making the headings boldface, using a sans serif font, and larger type than the rest of the text, but you do not divide the headings from the text. While you have distinguished the headings with typographical cues, you have not divided the headings from the text with white space. Thus, the typographical cues lose some of their effectiveness. Typographical cues clarify the spatial cues.

Figure 4 shows an example of a document that is typographically but not spatially cued.

The use of headings is a basic way to cue readers so they can scan the document for the information they need. Again, the integration of typographical and spatial cues is the most effective way to cue readers with headings. A boldfaced sans serif font that is larger than the rest of the text is an effective way to distinguish headings typographically. Then, separate the information with white space to frame and divide the headings from the text. If you have a hierarchy of headings, then you must distinguish between levels. This can be done by changing the type (smaller size as you go down the hierarchy) and the amount of space between headings (two spaces before and after the main heading and one space before and after second level headings). See Figure 5 for an example of cueing the reader with headings.

Figure 1. Document in a large block of text

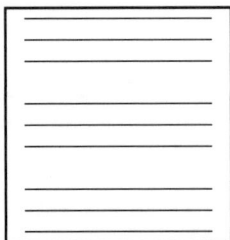

Figure 2. Document that is chunked by spatial changes

Figure 3. Document that is both spatially and typographically cued

Figure 4. Document that is typographically but not spatially cued

Main Heading

The main heading is a boldfaced 16 point sans serif font. There are two spaces that separate the main heading from the text.

Second Level Heading

The second level heading is in 14 point sans serif font. There is a space that separates the heading from the text.

Figure 5. Relationship of type and space in the use of headings

Subsequent levels of headings must be distinguished as well. You can continue to make the font smaller and also italicize it as well. Do not make the headings smaller in size than the text.

Another way in which space and type are related is leading. Leading (pronounced "ledding") is the amount of space between each line of text. The amount of space between lines of text can affect the document's readability. Figure 6 demonstrates the difference that leading has on the readability of a chunk of text.

Another effective tool for spatially cueing the reader is listing items instead of putting them into large chunks of text. There is a relationship between lists and content. Not all texts can be put into lists. Lists can be differentiated by the information they are presenting. Three different kinds of lists are as follows:

- Numbered lists should begin with numbers.
- Random lists of a series of elements can begin with bullets.

- Sequential list should begin with words like "first," "second," and "third."

Here are some general guidelines for lists:

- Lines in a list should be similar in length.
- Spacial cueing should frame the list (i.e., indented and right ragged).
- Turnovers (lines that carry over to another) should be aligned with the first line.

The contents of a list should not fit the format, but rather the format should facilitate the list.

Color

Like typographical and spatial cueing, color and typographical cueing are complementary. Color enhances the effectiveness of the type. The following are strengths of color cueing:

Too Little	Just Right	Too Much
Leading is the amount of space between each line of text. The amount of space between each line of text can affect the document's readability.	Leading is the amount of space between each line of text. The amount of space between each line can affect the document's readability.	Leading is the amount of space between each line of text. The amount of space between each line can affect the document's readability.

Figure 6. Leading

- Color draws the reader's attention.
- Color makes information easier to find.
- Color takes precedence over typographical cues.

Color cueing grabs the reader's attention and attracts the eye to the particular information that is colored. While the use of color can be an effective way to highlight information and attract the reader's attention, it also has its weaknesses. Too much color, like typographical cueing, can belie the purpose. If you use too much color to cue the reader, it can become distracting for the reader. In the case of coloring, less is more.

Color should be used sparingly, but you need to pick the appropriate information to distinguish. Save color for information that the reader could have a difficult time distinguishing. In other words, do not use color for headings if they can be effectively distinguished by type and space. Color can be effectively used for:

- Dividers between sections.
- Warnings to draw the reader's attention to a possible hazard.
- Hints for steps in a process or procedure.
- Keywords for quick referencing.

Finally, you should take into account the characteristics of the color itself. Below are three characteristics of color that you should consider before making a choice of color:

- Hue is the color.
- Value is the lightness or darkness of the color.
- Saturation is the intensity of the color.

These are important characteristics to consider because each has a role in the overall effectiveness of the color cue. For instance, lighter colors (yellow) are harder to read than darker colors (blue). Colors whose hue is closer in value to black are harder to distinguish as highlighters.

Summary

The integration of type, space, and color facilitates a better understanding of the information for the reader. They are not all separate items in the design of your document. Instead, they are complementary and should be used together to effectively cue the reader. Typographical cueing is influenced by spatial cueing. Contrasts in type and space frame specific information and make it more accessible to read. Color draws the reader's attention and should be used sparingly to maximize its effectiveness. Too much of all three can distract the reader and belie the intentions of the writer.

Document design is about making practical choices to help the reader. Type, space, and color are only a few of the decisions that affect the overall usability and appearance of a document. You may have to make decisions on the size and quality of paper you will use or whether to put a border around a particular body of text. These are all decisions that affect a document. Remember to always keep the reader in mind before, during, and after creating a document.

Document design should not be an afterthought, but an integral planning stage that will eventually affect the final document. A well-written document will lose its effectiveness if it is poorly designed and makes readers work to find the information they need. On the other hand, a well-designed document that is poorly written will also devalue the effectiveness of a document. Like type, space, and color, there is a synergism between design and text. They are not separate entities, but rather two interrelated entities that work together to create a document the reader can use.

Editing
a Document

Below is a document that contains pertinent information for the reader, but it is poorly designed. Recreate the document in a word processing program, using the three principles of document design that you just learned: type, space, and color. In a separate memo, explain to the instructor your choices.

While at work.

Before we open. As a College Station lifeguard, you are expected to show up to work 15 minutes before you are scheduled. When you arrive at work, make sure that the facility is ready to open to the general public. You should make sure all lifeguard stations have an umbrella and rescue tube, all mats are placed in potential slippery spots, the facility and parking lot is clean, all parties are set up, the chairs are unstacked, facility inspection is completed, and the slides are on. After you make sure the facility is ready to be opened, you should prepare yourself to go on-stand. You must have the proper uniform and equipment before you go on-stand. You should have the issued swim trunks/bathing suit, t-shirt if desired, a hat or visor, sunglasses, whistle, fanny pack with a pocket mask and dry gloves and gauze, and sunscreen at all times. You are responsible for the care and maintenance of your uniform. No variations of the uniform are allowed. Do not cut, tear, or deface you uniform. Defacing any part of your uniform will result in a verbal warning. Also, it is very important that you protect yourself from hazards. Sunscreen, a hat or visor, sunglasses, and a t-shirt (if desired) protect you from harmful UV rays. You must protect yourself from the potential risk of skin cancer! Make sure you are on-stand before we open for the general public.

On-stand. There is more to lifeguarding than sitting in the chair. While you on-stand, you should practice the 10/20 Second Rule, develop a scanning pattern that works best for you, scan the pool from top to bottom, avoid fixating or distractions, keep your eyes on the water at all times, be aware of the number of people in your zone, enforce the rules consistently and courteously, and maintain a professional appearance. You job as a lifeguard is to not only rescue people in need, but also to prevent accidents from happening. Lifeguard rotation.

The rotation system is very important, because you must maintain the ability to respond to any emergency in the zone while you are rotating with another incoming lifeguard. You must maintain alertness and cannot become distracted while rotating between lifeguard stations. Also, keep conversation between the incoming lifeguard to a minimum and only discuss pool-related topics. A rotation should be conducted as follows: incoming lifeguard reports to station, rescue tube is exchanged between lifeguards, incoming lifeguard watches zone and assumes responsibility, outgoing lifeguard climbs out of lifeguard chair, rescue tube is exchanged between lifeguards again, outgoing lifeguard watches zone and assumes responsibility, incoming lifeguard climbs into lifeguard chair, rescue tube is exchanged between lifeguards for the last time, incoming lifeguard watches zone and assumes responsibility, and finally the rotation is complete.

Part III
Worksheets

Student Profile

Last name: _____   Major: _____

First name: _____ (Indicate the name you want to go by in class)

Hometown: _____

1. Do you have special needs in the classroom (difficulty seeing the board or hearing, for example) you would like your instructor to be aware of?

2. Did your high school English classes emphasize primarily writing or literature?

3. Were you required to write a research paper in your high school English classes? Briefly describe the writing assignments required in the last high school English class you completed.

4. If you have completed college-level courses, what kinds of writing assignments were required in those courses?

5. Read the Preface to *Writing Traditions*. What are your expectations of English 104?

6. Briefly describe your strongest writing skills.

7. Briefly describe your weakest writing skills.

8. Have previous instructors given you rules or guidelines about writing that you usually try to follow? List these rules or guidelines below. Try to list a minimum of five.

9. Your signature on this profile indicates that you have been informed of and understand all course policies as well as your instructor's policies on major assignments, submission of late papers and attendance, and policies on plagiarism.

_____

Signature

_____

Date

Brainstorming

Name: _____ Section: _____ Date: _____

1. List three topics you are currently considering for a writing assignment:

2. For the topic you favor, write a paragraph that (a) explains why you selected the topic or (b) summarizes what you already know about the topic.

3. For the topic you favor, draft three questions you would like to answer in your reading and research.

4. Who will be your audience for this assignment?

5. For the topic you favor, write a paragraph that explains why this topic would be pertinent, relevant or timely for your designated audience.

Clustering

Name: _____   Section: _____   Date: _____

Use this sheet to do a clustering exercise on a topic of your choice. On the back of this sheet, use the ideas you generate to draft three tentative thesis statements. Then list three possible titles for a paper on this topic. Circle the thesis and title you will consider as your tentative thesis and title.

Clustering Exercise:

Tentative Thesis Statements:

Tentative Titles:

Analyzing a Topic #1

Name: _____ Section: _____ Date: _____

The first step in the research process for all of your assignments is selecting a topic that meets two requirements:

1. **The topic must be interesting.** Generally, writers who are interested in their topics have a good chance of making their topics interesting to readers.

2. **The topic must be researchable.** Trivial topics that might have popular interest but little serious scholarly interest are not appropriate for assignments in this course: for example, "The Best Places To Go during Spring Break" or "Britney and Justin: The Break-up." The topic must be old enough to have a substantial research base yet new enough to still be relevant and interesting. **Do not commit yourself to a topic if you are unsure about the availability of sources.** Find out how much material the library has on the topic.

Your instructor may ask you to avoid topics that are overworked—for example, steroids in sports, sports medicine, gun control, abortion, capital punishment, animal rights. In your class notes, record other topics your instructor asks you to avoid.

Directions: *Answer the following questions as thoroughly as possible.*

1. Briefly define or describe your research topic. Try to answer questions reporters usually ask—who? what? when? where? why?

2. What claim are you going to make about this topic? What is your thesis?

3. What is the scope of your topic? What are the main points you will discuss? List them below in their order of importance.

4. Are there points or issues you will need to omit in order to narrow your topic? What are they?

5. Give a brief account of what other people have said or written about your topic.

6. Explain why you agree or disagree with what other people have said about your topic.

7. Who is the audience for this essay? What aspects of the topic will be interesting and relevant to this audience?

8. What aspects of the topic may not be interesting or relevant to the audience?

9. Give a brief explanation of issues that might make your topic arguable or controversial.

10. Which of these issues will you emphasize in your essay? Explain why these issues seem relevant to your thesis.

11. Will you purposely avoid any of the issues? Explain why.

Analyzing a Topic #2

Name: _____   Section: _____   Date: _____

Directions: *Answer the following questions as thoroughly as possible.*

1. Briefly define or describe your research topic. Try to answer questions reporters usually ask—who? what? when? where? why? how?

2. What claim are you going to make about this topic? What is your thesis?

3. What is the scope of your topic? What are the main points you will discuss? List them below in their order of importance.

4. Are there any points or issues you will need to omit in order to narrow your topic? What are they?

5. Give a brief explanation of issues that might make your topic arguable or controversial.

Developing Your Thesis #1

Name: _____ Section: _____ Date: _____

The thesis of your paper is the main idea, the seed concept that generates the subject matter and sets limits on how much you will write. You should be able to state your thesis in a single declarative sentence, which may be further elaborated on in your introductory paragraph. If you explain and analyze the keywords of this sentence, you should be well on your way to developing the content for your paper.

Say, for example, that you have been asked to write on a topic of fast food. Your thesis is this: "While they are accused of deceptive advertising and making food irresistibly convenient and inexpensive, fast food producers should not be held responsible for the obesity of their customers." This sentence is rich in keywords: **fast food producers, accused, convenient, inexpensive, responsible, obesity, customers.** If you carefully define, explain, and qualify these terms, much of the work of your writing will be done.

For contrast, consider a much weaker thesis sentence: "Fast food doesn't make people obese." Or this one: "It is bad for people to eat fast food."

When it comes to drafting the paper itself, present a general statement of your thesis early in the paper. After you develop the concept thoroughly in the paper, you can restate the thesis with more precision and specificity in the conclusion.

Example: *Paper on Fast Food and Obesity Thesis statement in the introduction:* "While they are accused of deceptive advertising and making food irresistibly convenient and inexpensive, fast food producers should not be held responsible for the obesity of their customers."
Thesis statement in the conclusion: "The solution to obesity lies in the individual alone. Wisdom and morality, not legislation, can stop this weighty downward spiral."

1. In the space below, write three versions of a thesis statement for your next paper:

A.

B.

C.

2. In a group of two to four students, read and discuss your thesis statements, explaining the key words and indicating how you will develop the paper based on this thesis. Have your peers say which they think is the best version of the thesis.

3. Write the final version of your thesis below. It may be one of the original three, a combination of the features from several of them, or a totally new sentence. Explain briefly why you have chosen this sentence.

4. In the space below, write a short topic outline for your paper based on the thesis you have just developed.

5. With your writing partner or the members of your peer group, exchange thesis statements, but keep the outline you have written to yourself. Everyone should try writing a version of a short topic outline based on someone else's thesis.

In the space provided below, write your partner's thesis and a brief outline for his or her paper.

6. Compare and contrast the different outlines. How does your outline differ from the outline your writing partner wrote for your thesis? Which would be best? Why? Would you consider combining some of the features of each one? Discuss these questions in your group.

Developing Your Thesis #2

Name: _____   Section: _____   Date: _____

1. In the space below, write three versions of a thesis statement for your next paper:

A.

B.

C.

2. List below key words that appear in each version of your thesis.

3. Now write the final version of your thesis. It may be one of the original three, a combination of the features from several of them, or a totally new sentence. Explain briefly why you have chosen this sentence.

4. In the space below, write a short topic outline for your paper based on the thesis you have just developed.

Analyzing Your Perspective

Name: _____ Section: _____ Date: _____

Topic _____

1. What are some clichés, stereotypes, or truisms about your topic—standard ways of thinking that your fellow students are likely to associate with your subject matter?

2. What do you know about your topic that the majority of the class is not likely to know?

3. List some ways of interpreting or presenting your information that will stimulate your readers to look at the topic in a new way.

4. What initially interested you in your topic? A need to know more than you presently do? Concern for, or admiration or dislike of, the issues or individuals connected to it? A personal experience or situation that makes the topic interesting and relevant? Is this something that you can or should convey to your readers? (Remember, you do not want to convey bias, but it is good to convey passion and to encourage the reader's involvement in your topic.)

Analyzing an
Academic Audience

Name: _____ Section: _____ Date: _____

Topic _____

Directions: *Use the questions below to analyze your audience.*

1. Is your audience a general or specific academic audience? Are you writing to experts in one field or to scholars in many fields? Does your audience include students and staff at the university as well as professors?

2. What does your audience, presumably, already know about this topic?

3. What key terms will you define for your audience? List them and include a brief definition.

4. What kind of relationship do you want to establish with your audience: expert to expert? friend to friend? informed peer to uninformed peer? superior to subordinate? teacher to student? How will you go about establishing this relationship in your essay?

5. How will you make your topic interesting and relevant to the audience? What should they learn from your perspective of the issue that is new to them?

6. What is your overall aim? Do you want to inform your audience? Persuade your audience?

Essay Worksheet

Name: _____ Section: _____ Date: _____

Directions: *Use this copy of the Essay Worksheet to make copies to submit with each Writing Project. You should complete an essay worksheet after you have drafted a version of your paper for peer review. This worksheet will preface your peer review drafts when you organize supporting materials to hand in for grading.*

In a word or phrase, describe your topic:
In a word or phrase, give your working title:

Audience Analysis

1. In two to four sentences, describe your target audience indicated on your assignment prompt as specifically as your can. (i.e.; What is the average reading level of your audience? What do they know about your topic?)

2. In one sentence, tell what value your essay holds for its readers. How will they use it or benefit from it?

3. In one to two sentences, state (a) the purpose that you want to achieve in writing this essay for this specific audience and (b) the response you expect from this audience.

4. What actions/beliefs/decisions do you envision from your readers as a result of having read your essay? How will your essay motivate them?

Author

1. In a sentence, tell why you are an insider on this subject. In other words, why does your perspective matter on this topic?

2. In a word or phrase, identify the role you are playing as the author of this essay (that is, the persona you are assuming as the author).

3. What are some clichés, stereotypes, or truisms about your topic—that is, standard ways of thinking that your fellow students are likely to associate with your subject matter?

4. What do you know about your topic that the majority of the class is not likely to know?

5. List some ways of interpreting or presenting your information that will stimulate your readers to look at the topic in a new way.

Thesis Statement

1. In a complete sentence, state your thesis.

2. Write a short topic outline of your paper based on your thesis statement in the space provided below:

Analyzing Your
Audience #1

Name: _____   Section: _____   Date: _____

1. Give a brief explanation of your topic.

2. What does your audience know about this topic?

3. What key terms will you define for your audience? List them and include a brief definition.

4. What kind of relationship do you want to establish with your audience: expert to expert? friend to friend? informed peer to uninformed peer? superior to subordinate? teacher to student? How will you go about establishing this relationship in your essay?

5. How will you make your topic interesting and relevant to the audience?

6. What is your overall aim? Do you want to inform your audience? Persuade your audience?

7. In addition to your peers, what other audience might your essay have?

Analyzing Your
Audience #2

Name: _____   Section: _____   Date: _____

1. What does your audience know about the topic of your essay?

2. What should your audience know about your topic after reading your essay?

3. What key terms will you define for your audience? List them and include a brief definition.

4. What kind of relationship do you want to establish with your audience? expert to expert? friend to friend? informed peer to uninformed peer? superior to subordinate? teacher to student? How will you go about establishing this relationship in your essay?

5. How will you make your topic interesting and relevant to the audience?

6. What is your overall aim? Do you want to inform your audience? persuade your audience?

7. Explain how you will present your information in order to accomplish this aim. If your aim is primarily to inform, discuss your strategies—illustration, analogy, comparison and contrast, least important point to most important point, or chronological development, for example. If your aim is primarily to persuade, discuss how you will convince your audience to believe or to accept your point of view. Will your appeal be primarily to *ethos? logos? pathos?* Explain why you believe this strategy will be effective.

Understanding Context

Name: _____   Section: _____   Date: _____

Directions: *The context of a piece of writing is the historical and social background that you share with your readers. Below are some questions to help you think about your context and to accommodate in your writing special demands arising from the context. Answer each question as thoroughly as possible.*

1. Why is your topic important to readers at this time? In other words, how and why is your topic "timely" or "relevant"?

2. What factors in your own social background make the topic interesting to you or make you qualified to write about it?

3. What are the special social or historical attributes (social class, age, gender, generation, profession, educational level, etc.) of your particular audience—whether that audience is your teacher, your classmates, the general public, or some specific group?

4. How could the answers to questions 1, 2, and 3 affect the way you present the information? Will the context limit the kinds of arguments you can expect to succeed? What kinds of effects could it have upon your style, organization, or vocabulary?

Peer Critique
Guide #1

Name: _____ Section: _____ Date: _____

Directions: *Use this form to record your reactions as you listen to one of your peers read his or her papers during peer review. Use the back of the page to write a note to the author that suggests strategies for revising and improving the paper and points out the outstanding features of the paper that make it interesting, relevant, and effective.*

Like	Improve	Questions

Note to the Writer:

Content	Organizational Matters	Tone

Other comments:

Peer Critique
Guide #2

Name: _____ Section: _____ Date: _____

Assignment _____ Date_____

Name of Author _____ Section _____

Directions: *Use this form to record your reactions as you listen to one of your peers read his or her papers during peer review. Use the back of the page to write a note to the author that suggests strategies for revising and improving the paper and points out the outstanding features of the paper that make it interesting, relevant, and effective.*

Like	Improve	Questions

Note to the Writer:

Content	Organizational Matters	Tone

Other comments:

Critiquing and Reviewing the Work of Your Peers #1

Name: _____ Section: _____ Date: _____

Directions: *Use the following questions to discuss drafts of essays with one or two of your peers. As you work together, offer constructive suggestions and cite specific examples that make the essay effective or ineffective. Then respond in writing to the questions on the back of this page.*

Organization

- Would you evaluate the introduction as effective or predictable? Why? How could the writer improve the introduction?
- Would you evaluate the conclusion as effective or predictable? Why? How could the writer improve the conclusion?
- Does the paper include a thesis statement? Would you recognize this sentence as a thesis statement if the writer did not point it out to you by underlining or some other method?
- Do you find effective transitions within paragraphs and from one paragraph to another? Are transitions logical? predictable?

Development

- Does the writer include specific examples or illustrations to support all major points?
- Does the writer include statistics?
- Is the paper adequately developed?
- Does the writer include multiple perspectives on the topic?
- Does the paper ramble or suggest that the writer was more concerned with meeting the required number of pages than developing an effective paper?

Use of Sources

- How many sources are cited in the paper?
- Are the sources recent? dated?
- Are sources scholarly?
- Does the text refer to authors or their credibility, establishing authority?
- Are sources incorporated smoothly into the text?
- Do direct quotations appear at the end of paragraphs? Does the writer follow direct quotations with a comment emphasizing a major point? Which one of these uses of direct quotations seems to be more effective?

Audience Awareness

- In your opinion, would the intended audience find the paper interesting?
- In terms of style and diction, has the writer kept the audience in mind?
- Do you find passages that are confusing? garbled? ambiguous?

Meeting the Assignment

- Does the thesis establish the writer's position and aim?
- Does the writer use logical, ethical, or emotional appeals?
- Has the writer made adequate concessions?
- Has the writer ignored obvious perspectives?
- Has the writer followed a specific style correctly (MLA or APA, for example)?

Other Matters

- Does the paper offer good sentence variety?
- Does the writer avoid clichés? wordiness? word confusion?
- Would you characterize diction as crisp? predictable? inappropriate?
- Check the paper for surface errors (for example, spelling and typos, punctuation).

Reviewer's Analysis

- In the space below, list the strengths of the paper.
- In the space below, list your recommendations for revising and improving the paper.

Critiquing and Reviewing the Work of Your Peers #2

Name: _____   Section: _____   Date: _____

Title of the essay you are critiquing _____

Author of the essay you are critiquing _____

Directions: *As you answer the following questions, offer constructive suggestions and cite specific examples that make the essay effective or ineffective. You may not have time to discuss your responses with the writer, so make your written responses clear, and provide the type of response that you would find helpful.*

1. What is the writer's thesis?

2. Is the placement of the thesis effective or ineffective? Explain why.

3. Is the essay easily understood? Underline specific words or passages (for example, terms that need definition, generalizations, rambling sentences or paragraphs) that illustrate your response.

4. Is the prose consistent with academic discourse—that is, not overly informal? Cite three sentences that illustrate your response.

5. Describe the relationship the writer establishes with the audience and explain how the writer establishes this relationship.

6. Describe the presentational or organizational structure the writer has chosen—cumulative, chronological, or some other structure.

7. Does the writer use transitions effectively? Cite two examples to illustrate your response.

8. How many sources does the writer cite?

9. Which style of documentation does the writer use?

10. Has the writer provided appropriate documentation? If not, circle passages that require documentation.

11. Has the writer integrated quotations from sources effectively into the essay? Cite one example that illustrates your response.

12. Are quotations used effectively—that is, to illustrate or prove a point? If the writer seems to rely too much on quotations, do you find quoted passages that could be paraphrased? Mark these passages by writing "Try to paraphrase" in the margin.

13. Do you find problems with spelling, punctuation, or grammar that make the essay difficult to understand? Identify these for the writer with an asterisk. If time permits, discuss ways to remedy these problems.

14. Overall, does the essay seem to fulfill the assignment? Explain why or why not.

Writer's Analysis #1

Name: _____ Section: _____ Date: _____

1. In your opinion, what are the strengths of this paper? Be specific.

2. What difficulties did you encounter as you worked on this assignment?

3. In the space below, write your thesis statement.

4. List below topic sentences, in the order they appear in the paper, for paragraphs that support the thesis.

5. Write a brief summary (100–150 words) of your paper.

Writer's Analysis #2

Name: _____ Section: _____ Date: _____

1. In your opinion, what are the strengths of this paper? Be specific.

2. What difficulties did you encounter as you worked on this assignment?

3. In the space below, write your thesis statement.

4. List below topic sentences, in the order they appear in the paper, for paragraphs that support the thesis.

5. Write a brief summary (100–150 words) of your paper.

Revision
Strategies

Name: _____ Section: _____ Date: _____

Title of paper you are revising _____

When you revise a graded paper, you have an opportunity to rework the paper using your instructor's evaluation and suggestions as well as your own ideas for improving content, organization, and style. Your revised paper should illustrate **global revision**—that is, revision that goes beyond correcting only spelling, punctuation, or grammatical problems such as subject-verb agreement or comma splices. Before you begin revising, answer the following questions. Try to think of your instructor as an editor who will help you with drafts of the paper until it is ready to be submitted to your intended audience. The editor will find your strategies for revision interesting and helpful as he or she evaluates the revised paper, so be very specific as you answer each question.

1. Summarize your instructor's comments on the graded paper.

2. If you did not understand these comments or if you had questions about them, did you discuss the comments with the instructor? What was the outcome of the discussion?

3. Will the rhetorical situation change in any way? Consider in particular your role as the writer. Have you learned more about the subject since you submitted the paper to be graded? Have you changed your perspective?

4. After discussing your paper with another student in class, determine your strategy for revision and explain in detail in the appropriate spaces below. Will you revise primarily for content (adequate paragraph development, specific examples and illustrations), style (sentence variety, diction, active/passive voice), or organization paragraphs, specific thesis and topic sentences)?

Content:

Style:

Organization:

Analyzing Document Design

Name: _____ Section: _____ Date: _____

Directions: *Collect three advertisements from the school or local newspaper. Analyze the overall design of each advertisement by answering the following questions:*

- Who seems to be the targeted audience?
- How effective is the font used in the advertisement?
- Would another font be more effective? Why?
- Is there enough white space to frame and divide the information?
- If the advertisement is in color, is color used effectively?
- How does document design contribute to the overall effectiveness or ineffectiveness of the advertisement?

Use the space below to make notes. Be prepared to discuss your analysis in class. Attach the advertisements to this sheet.

Advertisement #1

Advertisement #2

Advertisement #3

Summarizing the Writing of Others

Name: _____   Section: _____   Date: _____

Directions: *Write summaries of the following passages. Your audience is your English class. (Bibliographical citations follow MLA style.)*

1. Kyle Field was born as a 400 × 400 foot all-purpose athletic area in the Spring of 1905. It would, however, take more than fencing and chalk lines to make Professor E. J. Kyle's vegetable patch playable ... That first year, only a few baseball games were played there as heavy rains and poor drainage forced the team to return to the drill field for home games. Undaunted, the Aggie nine handily won the state championship. Students and coaches banded together to level the field and pull the grass burrs. In fact, the students even donated the unused portion of their "breakage fee" to provide badly needed cash.

   After a few minor changes, including expanding the fenced area to 250,000 square feet, the field was ready for football. On October 7, 1905, A&M played its first football game on Kyle Field, defeating Houston Y.M.C.A. 29 to 0 (31).

   Chapman, David L. "Kyle Field Chronicle: Mules and Grandstands, Part II." *Texas Aggie*. July 1996: 31.

   Summary:

2. Historians will argue, and rightly so, that American women have been surrounded by contradictory expectations since at least the nineteenth century. My point is that this situation intensified with the particular array of media technology and outlets that interlocked in people's homes after WWII. It wasn't simply the sheer size and ubiquity of the media, although these, of course, were important. It was also the fact that the media themselves were going through a major transformation in how they regarded and marketed to their audiences that heightened, dramatically, the contradictions in the images and messages they produced. Radio, TV, magazines, popular music, film – these were the *mass* media, predicated on the notion of a national unified market, and their reason d'etre was to reach as many people as possible. To appeal to the "lowest common denominator," TV and advertisers offered homogenized romanticized images of America, which, especially under the influence of the cold war and McCarthyism, eschewed controversy and reinforced middle-class, sexually repressed, white-bread norms and values.

   Douglas, Susan. "Where the Girls Are." *Exchanges: Reading and Writing About Consumer Culture*. Eds. Ted Larner and Todd Lundberg. New York: Longman, 2001. 290–298.

Summary:

3. John Munroe Brazealle was denied his inheritance from his father's Mississippi estate because he lived in Mississippi. As the case law of the period shows, Brazealle, an emancipated slave, would have had a better chance of inheriting his father's estate had he lived elsewhere. The will of his white father was challenged in court on the grounds that Brazealle's deed of emancipation, executed in Ohio, was invalid according to Mississippi law. Consequently, it was argued that Brazealle was still a slave and as such could not inherit or own property. But as the judge's ruling demonstrates, the rights and privileges of this slave owner's son depended less upon Mississippi's emancipation laws than upon the jurisdiction in which he resided.

Mac Donald, Christine. "Judging Jurisdictions: Geography and Race in Slave Law and Literature of the 1830s." *American Literature* 71 : 4 (Dec. 1999): 625–655.

Summary:

4. On a separate sheet of paper, summarize one or two paragraphs from a source you are using for a paper, or an article from *The Battalion* and include an MLA citation of your source. Attach a copy of the source to your summary.

Quoting
and Paraphrasing

Name: _____ Section: _____ Date: _____

Directions: *Paraphrase the following passages. If an underlined sentence appears, it should be quoted and incorporated smoothly into your paraphrase. For example, to introduce a sentence that is a direct quotation from a passage by William O'Malley, you might write: According to O'Malley, "…" or O'Malley explains by saying, "…" Provide appropriate documentation for your paraphrase. Your audience is your English class. (Bibliographical citations follow MLA style.)*

1. Given the current general anger with corporate America because of the executive salaries, bonuses and stock options and layoffs and pay cuts for rank-and-file workers, there could hardly be a worse time for recent news stories to have revealed that many large companies take out life insurance policies on low-wage employees that allow them, literally, to profit from those employees' death.

   This so-called dead peasant, or dead janitor, insurance is purchased by companies on low-level employees, but when those employees die, their family receives no benefits. Instead, the money, all tax free, goes to the company, sometimes to fund executive compensation plans. Though perfectly legal, it is shockingly callous treatment of employees who typically receive paltry benefits compared to company executives and who usually are more vulnerable to termination or wage cuts and freezes during economic downturns.

   Loftis, Jack. "Grim Reaping." *Houston Chronicle* 27 April 2002: 34A.

   Paraphrase:

2. Mood rings were first seen as an extremely popular fad in the late 1970s, and they resurface regularly. The idea behind a mood ring is simple: Wear it on your finger and it will reflect the state of your emotions. The ring's stone should be dark blue if you're happy, and it supposedly turns black if you are anxious or stressed. While mood rings cannot reflect your mood with any real scientific accuracy, they actually are indicators of your body's involuntary physical reaction to your emotional state.

   The inside of the ring conducts heat from your finger to the liquid crystals in the "stone." The color green, which signifies "average" on the mood ring color scale, is calibrated to the surface temperature of a typical per- son, approximately 82 degrees Fahrenheit (28 degrees Celsius). If your surface temperature varies far enough from the norm, then the liquid crystals in the stone alter enough to cause a change in the color reflected.

"Question of the Day." *How Stuff Works*. Howstuffworks, Inc., 1998–2002. 6 May 2002 <http://www.howstuffworks.com/ question443. htm>.

Paraphrase:

3. As early as the first years of the 1940s, in the dying days of [Mae] West's employment by Hollywood, critics had slammed her last screen performances as <u>painfully old-fashioned and out of date</u>. A decade later, nothing had changed. West's infrequent stage appearances occasionally gained positive critical notice, but even the warmest treated her as an <u>irrelevant remnant of a distant past</u>. When West briefly returned to Broadway with a <u>Diamond Lil</u> revival in the late 1940s, she found herself labeled an "American institution," as beloved and indestructible as Donald Duck. <u>"She had become, in essence, a historical monument"</u>. As one critic put it, "Like Chinatown and Grant's Tomb, Mae West should be seen at least once."

The reasons for that sentiment are not hard to find. In part, they rested upon simple critical boredom. … Adding to the tedium, though few critics mentioned it, was the delicate matter of West's age. By the late 1940s she was well over fifty in a profession never kind to aging actresses, and aging sex symbols least of all.

Hamilton, Mary Beth. *When I'm Bad, I'm Better: Mae West, Sex and American Entertainment*. New York: HarperCollins, 1995. 238.

Paraphrase:

Recognizing Plagiarism

Name: _____ Section: _____ Date: _____

Directions: *The passage below is taken from an extended description of nineteenth century London by Daniel Pool. In* What Jane Austen Ate and Charles Dickens Knew, *he discusses many aspects of every day nineteenth-century life that might not be familiar to contemporary readers. Read the excerpt and the passages that follow it. Then determine whether the passages would be considered plagiarism or fair and ethical use of sources. Underline any passages that rely on the phrasing of the original source.*

Original Passage

 The fog in London was very real. Just why it was the color it was no one has ever been able to ascertain for sure, but at a certain time of the year—it was worst in November—a great yellowness reigned everywhere, and lamps were lit inside even during the day. In November, December, and January the yellow fog extended out some three or four miles from the heart of the city, causing "pain in the lungs" and "uneasy sensations in the head." It has been blamed in part on the coal stoves. At eight o'clock in the morning on an average day over London, an observer reported the sky began to turn black with the smoke from thousands of coal fires, presumably for morning fires to warm dining rooms and bedrooms and to cook breakfast. Ladies going to the opera at night with white shawls returned with them gray. It has been suggested that the black umbrella put in its appearance because it did not show the effects of these London atmospherics. The fog was so thick, observed a foreigner at mid-century, that you could take a man by the hand and not be able to see his face, and people literally lost their way and drowned in the Thames. In a very bad week in 1873 more than 700 people above the normal average for the period died in the city, and cattle at an exhibition suffocated to death.

Pool, Daniel. *What Jane Austen Ate and Charles Dickens Knew.* New York: Simon and Schuster, 1993. 30.

Passage #1

According to historian Daniel Pool, yellow fog was a major problem for citizens of London in the nineteenth century, but no one knew why it was particularly bad in the month of November or, for that matter, why it was yellow. In the late fall and early winter months, the fog even affected people living a few miles outside of the city, causing people to experience "pain in the lungs" and "uneasy sensations in the head" (30). One theory holds coal stoves responsible. In the city, the sky began turning dark as early as 8:00 am because of smoke from fires that were necessary to warm houses and cook meals. The fog was so dense that it was known to blacken white clothing and made it difficult to see very far. Pool reports that "people literally lost their way and drowned in the Thames" because of it (30). He claims that "in a very bad week in 1873 more than 700 people above the normal average for the period died in the city, and cattle at an exhibition suffocated to death" (30).

Passage #2

In the nineteenth century, in the city of London yellow fog reigned everywhere and lamps were lit inside even during the day—sometimes as early as 8:00 in the morning on an average day. It was much worse in November than any other time of the year. Sometimes the yellow fog extended out some three or four miles from the heart of the city. A lot of the problem was blamed on coal stoves. The smoke from these stoves was so bad that it messed up ladies' white evening gloves. One foreigner observed that the fog was so thick, that you could take a man by the hand and not be able to see his face, and people literally lost their way and drowned in the Thames (Pool 30).

Passage #3

The London fog wasn't the stuff of literary imagination. It was real and it caused many problems, especially in November. Just why it was the color that it was no one has ever been able to really explain, but it was so yellow that a great yellowness reigned everywhere in the fall and lamps had to be lit even in the daytime. The problem extended out some three or four miles from London, causing discomfort for people who had lung problems and headaches, too. Coal stoves were probably the source of the problem. At eight o'clock in the morning on an average day in the city, an observer reported the sky began to turn black from the smoke of thousands of coal fires used in the morning to warm dining rooms and bedrooms. Ladies going to the opera got their clothes dirty just by going outside. Some historians credit the appearance of the black umbrella to this period. They made it black because it didn't show the effects of the London atmosphere. The fog was so thick that lots of people stumbled into the Thames and drowned. In one of the worse episodes in 1873, 700 people died in the city and cattle suffocated to death, too (Pool 30).

Passage #4

Daniel Pool tells us that the fog in London was very real. Just why it was the color it was no one has ever been able to determine for sure, but at a certain time of the year—it was worst in November—a great yellowness could be found everywhere, and lamps were lit inside even during the day. According to Pool, in November, December, and January the yellow fog extended out some three or four miles from the heart of the city, causing "pain in the lungs" and "uneasy sensations in the head" (30). It has been blamed in part on the coal stoves. At eight o'clock in the morning on an average day over London, according to Pool, an observer reported the sky began to turn black with the smoke from thousands of coal fires, presumably for morning fires to warm dining rooms and bedrooms and to cook breakfast. Pool also tell us that ladies going to the opera at night with white shawls returned with them gray. He even suggests that the black umbrella put in its appearance because it did not show the effects of these London atmospherics. He ends his account of this problem with the following observation: "In a very bad week in 1873 more than 700 people above the normal average for the period died in the city, and cattle at an exhibition suffocated to death" (30).

MLA Bibliography Exercise

Name: _____ Section: _____ Date: _____

Directions: *Write bibliographic citations for the following sources using the MLA style of documentation. You may attach a separate sheet of paper for your answers.*

1. A book published by the Mississippi University Press entitled *Unveiling Kate Chopin*, by Emily Toth, a Chopin scholar. The book, 290 pages long, was published in Jackson, Mississippi in 1999.

2. An article entitled "New Beutel Director Looks to Improve Health Center," written by Sarah Darr, appearing in *The Battalion* on Friday, April 26, 2002, beginning on page 1 and continuing on page 2.

3. An online article in Daily News section of *People* online. The article is titled "Harry Potter Author Misses Deadline," and the author is Stephen M. Silverman. The URL is http://people.aol.com/people/news/now/0,10958,235517,00.html>. The date of publication and access is May 6, 2002.

4. "Listen, Spot," by *Time* writer Bill Barol, which appeared in the 159th volume, number 18, on May 6 2002.

5. A personal interview you have conducted with one of your professors. You supply the date and time.

6. A book review of David Salsburg's *The Lady Tasting Tea*, the reviewer is Tim Whitley. The review appears in the *Journal of Chemical Education*, volume 78 number 12, in the year 2001, and is printed on only page 1599. This journal uses continuous pagination.

7. The introduction to the sixth edition of *A World of Ideas: Essential Readings for College Writers*, a book published in 2002 by Bedford, which is an imprint of St. Martin's in Boston. The introduction, written by the book's editor, Lee A. Jacobus, appears on pages 1–18.

8. An essay by Deborah Tannen, "Sex, Lies and Conversation," on pages 307–313 of the fourth edition of *The Longwood Reader*, edited by Edward A. Dornan and Charles W. Dawe. This book was published in 2000 in Boston by Allyn and Bacon.

9. Lyrics for Elton John's "The One" copyright 1992, from the compact disc *The One*, which was distributed by MCA in Canada.

10. A recipe for "Bean and Rice Salad," which is included on a CD-ROM entitled *Kitchen Gourmet: 5000 Delicious Recipes*. The CD-Rom was produced by SoftKey Multimedia, Inc., in 1996, and is Windows-compatible.

APA Bibliography Exercise

Name: _____ Section: _____ Date: _____

Directions: *Write bibliographic citations for the following sources using the APA style of documentation. You may attach a separate sheet of paper for your answers.*

1. A book published by the University of Edinburgh Press in 1993 entitled *The Humanism of Milton's Paradise Lost*, by David Reid. The book is 186 pages long.

2. Lyrics from the Sundays' song "Summertime" (copyright 1997). The song is from the compact disc *static & silence*, produced by Geffen Records, a division of Warner Brothers Records, Inc., in Los Angeles, California, and is distributed by Universal Music & Video Distribution, Inc.

3. An article from *Entertainment Weekly* by David Browne, titled "The Price is Right." The article appeared on their web page on May 6, 2002, URL <http://www.ew.com/ew/article/commentary/ 0,6115,235236~10~0~whatsup-withthose,00.html>.

4. "The Fish," a poem by Marianne Moore. Found in *Literature: A Pocket Anthology*, on page 708. This anthology was edited by R.S. Gwynn for Penguin Academics, published in 2002 by Longman, which is an imprint of Addison Wesley Longman, Inc., in New York.

5. A quote from James Strachey's introduction to Sigmund Freud's *The Interpretation of Dreams*. The book is a reprint; it was first published by Avon Books in 1965 in New York, and in this instance it is published by Bard, an imprint of Avon, in 1998 in New York. The quote is from page xvi.

6. An article from *College English*, "Hope, for the Dry Side" by Bette Lynch Husted. This journal has continuous pagination, and the article appeared on pages 243–249, volume 69 number 2, November 2001, Santa Clara, California.

7. A videotape of *Dead Poets Society*, which was distributed by Buena Vista Home Video in 1989. The film stars Robin Williams and was produced by Steven Haft, directed by Peter Weir, and written by Tom Schulman. Buena Vista Home Video is located in Burbank, California.

8. A personal interview you conducted with one of your professors. You decide when and where it took place.

9. An article appearing Summer 2000, "Psychiatry and Postmodern Theory," by Bradley Lewis in the *Journal of Medical Humanities*, volume 21 number 2, pages 71–84.

10. A newspaper article, "Student Teachers Find Job Market Favorable" by Salatheia Bryant. Printed in the *Houston Chronicle* on page 29A and 30A, on Saturday, April 27, 2002.

Analyzing Prose Style

What Is Style?

How you define *style* depends upon your perspective:

- For the writer, style involves the *decisions* (conscious or unconscious, principled or intuitive) about what kinds of words to choose and sentences to construct.
- For the reader, style involves the *effects* created by certain combinations of words and sentences.
- For the text (or the textual analyst, or literary critic), style comprises the *patterns and relations* of words and sentences.
- For the language as a whole (or the linguist), style represents the means by which individual writers, readers, and texts emerge within, among, and against the conventions of usage and syntax that define the language and the social world.

What Can You Do with Style?

A writer can use style to:

- bring himself or herself into being (to "express" oneself or "construct" a persona)
- communicate with others (not only persuade, but make connections of all kinds)
- practice the craft of writing (to make a beautiful or workable thing)
- fulfill the destiny of a language-using, social life-form (to be human)
- change the world (by making a historical record of experiences and ideas)

A Deviation from a Norm

Style may best be defined as something new—*a deviation from a conventional norm for the purpose of emphasis or impact*. The worksheets on the following pages help you to explore the concept of style as a deviation from a norm.

A Method for Stylistic Analysis

1. Imagine that there is a normal language. For example, say that *every sentence should have a simple, active narrative structure* (subject-verb-[complement], as in "The kid ate the grass") and that *every word should be used only according to a single denotative meaning, such as the first one given in the dictionary* ("kid" means only a young goat, not a small human child).

   Now list every *deviation* from this norm that you can find in the passage you are analyzing.

1a. (optional) If you know the technical name for the deviation ("complex sentence," "inverted subject and verb," "passive voice," "metaphor," "oxymoron," etc.), put it in your list.

2. For every deviation, list at least two other ways of communicating what the author seems to be saying. Try to use "normal" language for one alternative. Then create another deviant alternative.

3. Finally, speculate on why the author may have decided to use the original deviation. Reflect on the ways that the style

   - brings the author to life,
   - communicates or fails to communicate (including or excluding a particular readership),
   - creates beauty,
   - performs a social or cultural function,
   - and attempts to make an historical impact.

On the next page is a sample analysis. It does not even begin to exhaust the deviations in the passage but merely selects a few. On the empty table on the page following the sample, list a few of the deviations omit-ted in the sample analysis; then complete the analysis yourself. After the sample, there are other passages and tables for you to practice with.

Sample Analysis of Prose Style

PASSAGE FOR ANALYSIS:

Like the network of new highways proposed for the canyon country, these power plants are meant not for current needs but for "anticipated" needs. "Planning for growth," it's called. The fact that planning for growth encourages growth, even forces growth, would not be seen as a serious objection by the majority of Utah-Arizona businessmen and government planners. They believe in growth. Why? Ask any cancer cell why it believes in growth.

—Edward Abbey, "Canyonlands and Compromises," 1971.

Deviant Word, Phrase, or Sentence	Normal Alternative	Deviant Alternative	Purpose or Effect of Author's Style
"network of new highways" (metaphor)	"many new highways"	"web of new highways"	Unlike "web," which connotes something natural, "network" suggests an elaborate technological system.
"are meant not for current needs but for 'anticipated needs'" (passive voice, inversion of positive and negative complements, use of quotation marks)	"the developers intend to meet anticipated needs, not current needs"	"the developers care nothing about the needs of the people and the land in its present state but want only to create needs that have to be satisfied in the future"	Passive voice allows the writer to put "roads" in the subject position for emphasis and cohesion with previous sentence; the inversion puts "anticipated needs" at the end of the sentence so that it can be explained further in the next sentence; the quotation marks distance the author from the quoted phrase, creating irony.
"Planning for growth," it's called. (inversion of complement, quotation, contraction, substitution of expletive "it" for agent in subject position)	"The developers call the process of meeting anticipated needs 'planning for growth.'"	"'Planning for growth' is the terminology used by the developers."	Putting the complement first makes the transition to the previous sentence; quotation sets up the troublesome phrase to be interpreted later in the passage; the contraction creates an informality typical of the persona (the natural man); the omission of the agent keeps the focus on the idea of "growth," which is being criticized.

Name: _____   Section: _____   Date: _____

Complete the analysis in this table:

Deviant Word, Phrase, or Sentence	Normal Alternative	Deviant Alternative	Purpose or Effect of Author's Style

Name: _____ Section: _____ Date: _____

PASSAGE FOR ANALYSIS:

Though passion may have strained, it must not break our bonds of affection. The mystic chords of memory, stretching from every battle-field, and patriot grave, to every living heart and hearthstone, all over this broad land, will yet swell the chorus of the Union, when again touched, as surely they will be, by the better angels of our nature.

—Abraham Lincoln, First Inaugural Address, 1861.

Deviant Word, Phrase, or Sentence	Normal Alternative	Deviant Alternative	Purpose or Effect of Author's Style

Name: _____ Section: _____ Date: _____

Passage for Analysis:

What kind of people came to the Panhandle? Dry farmers, moving with a rainy season and hanging on stubbornly once that season was past. Land and oil speculators, railroad developers, opportunity seekers (the heirs of the first gold seekers), Union Army deserters, the religious and the reprobate—they came seeking not Eden but wilderness rich for shaping. Or they came knowing only what it was they did not want, seeking for—what, they did not know.

—A. G. Mojtabi, *Blessed Assurance: At Home with the Bomb in Amarillo, Texas*, 1986.

Deviant Word, Phrase, or Sentence	Normal Alternative	Deviant Alternative	Purpose or Effect of Author's Style

Part IV
Student Papers

Assignments

The sample papers that follow illustrate achievements of student writers in English 104. Space does not allow us to include the invention exercises, multiple drafts, and peer review copies each writer generated during the process of writing his or her paper. What you will find here are the papers students submitted for grading. Brief descriptions of the assignments for these papers are included as well. All of the assignments specified either a general academic audience (faculty and students) or a scholarly journal as the writers' intended audience.

While these assignments may differ somewhat from the assignments your instructor makes, you should find the student papers valuable for class discussion. They are not models for you to imitate. They were selected because they illustrate (1) strengths writers bring to college composition courses and (2) problems writers frequently encounter as they draft and revise papers for specified groups of readers. Instead of playing guessing games about grades these papers received, concentrate on analyzing how each writer achieves his or her purpose. Pay special attention to both global and sentence-level matters. As you read the papers, consider how each writer handles audience analysis, introductions and conclusions, transitions, execution of ideas, argument, documentation, and synthesis of sources. And come to class ready to explain how you would respond to this paper if you had the opportunity to offer a peer critique.

Report on a Current Event or Issue

Paper #1, "A Mexican-American Crisis," is a response to an assignment that asked students to

- select a current event or issue,
- summarize the event or issue,

- quote the reactions and evaluations of popular and academic sources, and
- state their responses to their sources.

This assignment also states: *Your aim is primarily to inform your readers; however, your paper may have a persuasive edge if your summary and response encourage readers to rethink or reconsider their understanding of the event or issue you've discussed.*

Analyzing and Interpreting an Urban Legend

In Paper #2, "Legends of Hope Born Out of Terrorism," the writer analyzes an urban legend as a cultural symbol and social or moral instrument. The assignment includes the following explanation of the writer's purpose: *You should be able to write a coherent, grammatically correct essay that analyzes one or more urban legends. You will propose what types of social and cultural symbols are present and integrate the core text into your essay and other sources as appropriate. Your paper should cite, quote, summarize, and paraphrase other writer's ideas and words. It should also demonstrate your ability to analyze data and to read critically.*

Position Paper

"Exploring the Vast Inequality of Women in the Workplace," Paper #3, is an example of a position paper. Students selected arguable topics that would be of interest to the academic community and took a stance on the topic. The assignment explained that the aim of the paper was to persuade readers.

The Extended Research Paper

Paper #4, "Acknowledging a Dead President: John F. Kennedy's Memorable Policies," is an extended Assignments 97 research paper that required the writer to use an effective conceptual design to synthesize, analyze, and interpret information from paper and electronic sources. The assignment included the following directions: The paper should

1) *demonstrate a thorough understanding of the various perspectives surrounding an issue, especially those in opposition to your own, and*

2) *argue your perspective or opinion on an issue, using the research you've gathered to provide relevant background information and to aid in development of your argument.*

Global Revision

Paper #5, "Gas Shortage: The Big Picture," is a revision of a paper written early in the semester. The assignment for Paper #5 asked students to rethink, rework, and revise—and, if they chose, reformat—one of their papers, making it a "showcase for their work". The assignment also outlined requirements for global revision: *The revised paper will be a coherent, grammatically correct essay that incorporates one new source, addresses a new audience, and quotes, summarizes, and paraphrases other writers' ideas and words.* You'll find the student's paper and the revised version as well.

PAPER #1

Elizabeth Lara

Rebecca Caldwell

English 104

9 October 2001

A Mexican-American Crisis

The minimum wage in Mexico is about eighty cents an hour. Many multinational corporations have transferred to Mexico to take advantage of these low wages, building a twin plant in Mexico to compliment a plant in the United States. The twin plant, a *maquiladora*, enables a company to make use of cheap labor. They have become so popular that there are over 3,000 in Mexico. These maquiladoras should be abolished because they exploit cheap labor and have harsh working conditions.

The Handbook of Texas Online describes the maquiladora as "an industrial plant that assembles imported mechanisms into products that can be exported." The parts made are usually parts needed for assembly in manufacturing plants in the United States. The idea behind maquiladoras is that a United States or European company transfers one or many of its manufacturing plants to a low cost country. Maquiladoras operate at low costs in places where the currency is weaker than the dollar. Since Mexico's currency, the peso, is low in value, a U.S. company can exchange their currency for pesos and pay their workers and business expenses. When the U.S. company's products are sold, they are sold in dollars and make a vast profit.

One of the major problems with cheap labor in maquiladoras is the low wages for workers. A Mexican worker in a maquiladora doing the same job as an American worker in an American corporation is paid much less. According to "Sweatshops by Any Other Name–Maquiladoras" a Mexican worker is paid between $0.80 and $1.25 an hour.

Unless the value of the peso increases, workers in maquiladoras will never be paid a decent wage. A wage increase could enable them to keep up with the cost of living. An online article, "Maquiladora Workers Demand a Living Wage," quotes a maquiladora worker in Tijuana speaking out about cheap labor: "I know these U.S. corporations are taking advantage of the low wages here, and we desperately need these jobs, but they should pay us enough to live and eat decently and send our children to school." As this article points out, workers are not well compensated for their jobs and when they try to form unions, they are either penalized or fired.

Another problem resulting from cheap labor is harsh working conditions. The working environment is unsafe and unsanitary. In "A Catastrophe Waiting to Happen," David Bacon reports that two-dozen workers testified in San Diego and stated that "overhead cranes carry truck chassis weighing a tone or more through the plant. Their controls malfunction and a crane once dropped a chassis, narrowly missing workers below." These workers also stated that deep pools of water covered the floor in some departments during heavy rainfall and heavy cables, some with frayed insulation that carry 480 volts, snake through the water to industrial arc-welders. It is hard to believe that these working conditions are legal under the North American Free Trade Agreement. Inspectors in these maquiladoras should have noted the conditions and tried to eliminate them. If a company in the United States had a severe working environment, inspectors would shut them down. It is only right that United States companies in Mexico keep a safe environment for their workers. In the same testimonial reported by David Bacon, workers reported that bathrooms were unsanitary: "One toilet stall door had fallen off … there was no toilet paper or hot water … the sinks worked so poorly that they generate many biological organisms." Unsanitary bathrooms are hazardous to a person's health and could cause the poor workers to fall ill or develop diseases. All of these conditions are common in most, if not all, maquiladoras.

Most maquiladora workers are desperate for work to keep themselves and their families alive. American businesses know that and they are taking advantage of the fact that they can get away with paying their laborers close to nothing. What will happen in the years to come? What if the peso continues to drop? The answer is that working conditions will become worse and wages will get smaller. American entrepreneurs will still get their money and the world will continue to turn as if this problem never existed.

Works Cited

Bacon, David. "Han Young—A Catastrophe Waiting to Happen." 2 March 1998. 5 October. 2001.
    <www.igc.org/dbacon/mexico/05hanyng.html>

"Maquiladora Workers Demand a Living Wage." *Cross Border Connection*. October 1996. 5 October. 2001 <www.igc.org/trac/feature/planet/maria/html>

Sargent, John. "Maquiladoras and Skill Development." *Journal of Borderland Studies*. Volume XII
    (1997) numbers 1 & 2. 5 October. 2001 <www.absborderlands.org/journal97.html>

"Sweatshops by any Other Name—Maquiladoras." 5 October 2001. <www.globalexchange.org/
    education/ california/dayofthedead.html>

"The Maquiladoras." January 1995. 5 October 2001 <www.sfsu.edu/~jdrew/web/maquila.html>

Wilson, Patricia A. "Maquiladoras." *The Handbook of Texas Online*. 23 July 2001. 5 October 2001
    <www.tsha.utexas.edu/handbook/online/articles>

PAPER #2

Courtney Abbott

English 104–512

Miss Trayers

7 March 2002

Legends of Hope Born Out of Terrorism

Throughout American history, times of trouble have often been accompanied by stories of survival and overcoming great odds. These urban legends serve as an outlet for a wounded society to boost morale and lift spirits in trying times. After the terrorist attacks on the World Trade Center and the Pentagon on September 11, a suffering America found comfort in such stories, which began to circulate shortly after the attacks.

One such story was that of Daisy, the seeing eye dog whose owner, James, worked on the 101 floor of the first tower in the World Trade Center. According to the legend, after the plane hit the tower, James, knowing he would not make it out of the building, took Daisy off of her harness so she could make it to safety. Instead of heading down the stairs to escape the collapsing building, Daisy went up the stairs and soon returned with James' boss and a large group of people (Beaudoin).

Daisy entered the burning building twice more; the third time, the building collapsed while she was inside. She was carried out this time by a fireman who said she led the men right to the people before being injured. According to Jake Beaudoin, she "suffered acute smoke inhalation, severe burns on all four paws, and a broken leg, but she saved 967 lives" (Beaudoin). The heroic tale of Daisy the life-saving seeing eye dog is just one example of the stories created, or perhaps even of memories exaggerated, that people tend to cling to in times of trouble. Daisy's tale happens to be strikingly similar to an article entitled "Faithful Dog Leads Blind Man 70 Floors Down WTC Just Before Tower Collapses." Published online, this article is about a dog named Dorado:

> According to the contra Costa Times report published today [Omar Eduardo] Rivera described how he unleashed his faithful friend, so that the dog might escape. But despite the chaos and the crowds of fleeing people, the four-year-old Labrador Retriever suppressed any selfish instinct for survival and instead stayed by the man's side and guided him to safety.

Whether or not the stories are truth, exaggeration, or fiction matters little in respect to the need for such tales as an integral part of the healing process. Such legends are proof to victims that there is still goodness left in the world, even amidst so much hatred and ruin. These uplifting messages are a necessity to a society suddenly burdened by death, destruction, and, consequently, fear of more to come.

It is also significant to note that these and many stories circulating after September 11 are about animals, or, more specifically, about dogs. The role of the canine remains unchanged throughout recent history; dogs have long been considered "man's best friend," due in part to their loving and loyal nature towards man. It is understandable, therefore, that the stories feature dogs not only as pets, but also as nurturers and lifelong companions to their owners. The dogs take on a humanlike persona, showing characteristics of bravery, courage and determination in the face of crisis. Many people realize the loving relationship between dog and owner, and the stories' use of this bond makes the reader emotionally attached and sympathetic to the plot.

This type of urban legend also reinforces people's faith in their particular god or religion. For instance, one story tells of a search-and-rescue worker who, while rummaging through the charred rubble of the Pentagon in the days following the attack, looked up and saw a stool sitting, untouched, very near where one of the jets had crashed. On the stool was an open bible, free of any burn marks or damage in or within several feet of it. Rumors of War: Bible Study quotes the soldier who reacted commented on this story: "I'm not as religious as some, but that would have me thinking. I just can't explain it."

Some take such tales as a sign that there exists a higher power beyond their control. Others see them as a reinforcement of their faith and renewed hope in humanity. As for those who lost family friends or coworkers to the attacks, this and other stories provide reassurance that, although their loved ones are no longer with them, they are in a better place.

These emotion-packed stories are therapeutic in nature and are designed to be emotionally and spiritually uplifting to readers, especially to those who have recently suffered great traumatic experiences, such as the terrorist attacks on September 11. They are simply vessels of hope, comfort, and reassurance at a very unstable time in life, and although they may not be entirely factual, such urban legends contribute a great deal to the healing process.

Works Cited

Beaudoin, Jacob. email message. 25 Feb. 2002 <jake_beau@gmx.net>.

"Rumors of War: Bible Study." 24 Feb. 2002 <http://www.snopes2.com/rumors.bible.htm>

"Faithful Dog Leads Blind Man 70 Floors Down WTC Just Before Tower Collapses." Volume II,

    Issue 3. 14 Sept. 2001 <http://www.dogsinthenews.com/issues/0109/articles/010914a.htm>

PAPER #3

Michelle Henry

Rebecca Caldwell

English 104–512

October 10, 2001

Exploring the Vast Inequality of Women in the Workplace

Why is it that feminists are stereotyped as loud groups of angry women picketing in front of buildings and chanting for equal rights? *Webster's* definition of feminism as "advocacy of increased political activity of right for women" does not fully account for these fanatical activists (260). The stereotypical picketers described above are the more extreme feminists who make the silent people working to improve labor conditions for women look bad. Women around the world, not just in America, constantly face discrimination in the workplace, ranging from lower pay rates to sexual harassment and prejudice.

In "Gender Wage Discrimination," Gail Schaffer writes that "seventy percent of Americans believe that women … are paid less than men for doing the same work." In many cases, women perform the same tasks as their coworkers and do so within the same amount of time, yet don't see the same amount of income as men. On average, an American family loses four thousand dollars per year to this "wage gap," which collectively adds up to an annual loss of 200 billion dollars in America alone (Schaffer). Gene Koretz, writing for *Business Week*, claims that both women and men "feel that women will accept lower pay than men and that women are more malleable in a bargaining situation," which may be a reason that women's pay rates are lower than men's (34). And Darrell Geddes cites a current population survey that reveals that women "earn[ed] 72 percent of the average male worker's wage" in 1995. This survey also shows an increase in women's wages since 1969 when women's wages were only 56 percent of men's, so American society, with respect to women's rights, is slowly heading towards equality.

America is not the only society in which women are treated unfairly in the workplace. Throughout the world, women constantly face prejudice in their lives. In the United Kingdom, the chairwoman of the equal opportunities commission, Julie Mellor, made the comment that young women "are already earning 10 percent less than their male colleagues by the age of 20" and that these young women are "less likely ever to reach the top of their field of work" (Carvel). Even in Sweden, "women earn 15 to 20 percent less than men" (Ornerborg 23). Across the globe, sex is a common factor in the hourly pay rates of working women, causing them to be paid less than their equally qualified coworkers.

In addition to the worldwide difference in income for men and women, sexual harassment and prejudice are common issues among women. Albert Hunt estimates that "about 44 percent of women feel they have been discriminated against because of gender … and almost a third say they have been sexually harassed." The problem of sexual harassment, compounded by sexual prejudice, represses the advancement of women in the workplace. Because of prejudice, women face problems in working towards the top of their fields. They are seen as emotional and less forceful, and—as a result—are often not recognized as authority figures. Because of this, women miss out on many opportunities that men receive. There may never be a solution to sexual harassment and prejudice; the problems may become less frequent, but they will always be issues women struggle with.

Sexual harassment, the lack of opportunities, and unequal pay rates are just a few of the problems women must face in their daily lives. Many cases of sexual discrimination have yet to be discovered, since the majority of employers frown upon the discussion of wages among employees. While the argument that workers should be able to know whether or not their wages are proportional to others is a completely different topic, it is clear that "working women deserve the respect and dignity of being paid fairly, and their families deserve the wages they are being denied because of persistent wage discrimination" (Schaffer). There is absolutely no reason why women should be treated as inferior to men in a place of employment. In "Employment Equity: Some Career Issues," Donald Diubaldo explains that "despite the gains that have been made in employment equity in recent years, women may still feel a need for further progress" (8). Gender discrimination in the workplace must be stopped if the goal of an egalitarian world is ever to be reached.

Works Cited

Carvel, John. "Girl Power Generation Faces Workplace Shock." 20 July 2001. 30 Sept 2001. http://education.guardian.co.uk.

Diubaldo, Donald. "Employment Equity: Some Career Issues." *Guidance & Counseling* 9 (1994): 8–11.

Geddes, Darryl. "Inequality Among Women in the Workplace is Widening." 19 Feb 1998. 30 Sept 2001. http://www.news.cornell.edu.

Hunt, Albert R. "Women See Progress, but Also Inequity." n.d. 30 Sept 2001. http://www.imdiversity. com.

Koretz, Gene. "She's a Woman, Offer Her Less." *Business Week* 7 May 2001: 34

Morehead, Albert and Loy Morehead. "Feminism." *The New American Webster Handy College Dictionary.* 1995 ed.

Ornerborg, Elisabet. "Sweden: Court Battles for Equal Pay." *Unseco Courier* (2000): 23–24.

Shaffer, Gail S. "Gender Wage Discrimination." *FDCH Congressional Testimony.* 8 June 2000.

PAPER #4

Hank Hollywood

Instructor's name

English 104.513

8 Dec. 1997

Acknowledging a Dead President: John F. Kennedy's Memorable Policies

John F. Kennedy is remembered for his tragic death in Dallas, Texas, on November 22, 1963. It is important to look past his assassination and see the policies he enacted while President. Kennedy established a name for himself with such issues as the Bay of Pigs, the Cuban missile crisis, the civil rights movement, and his personal war on organized crime in the United States. The assassination brings all these issues to the forefront because it is believed by some historians, politicians, and friends that some of these controversial events may have eventually led to his death. I believe that to give justice to the Kennedy legacy, we, the American people, have to understand the issues and policies he had to address during his short lived presidency. The loss of Kennedy deprived America of great leadership, and it left the question of whether or not the young ambitious President left a mark on American history. I believe President Kennedy was a very instrumental figure in American history, and it is also my belief that his policies should be remembered, rather than his death.

Presidents are usually remembered in history for issues or policies that they enacted, but these are not always positive experiences; Kennedy came close to having such a humiliating disaster during his first week in the White House. In 1961 the Central Intelligence Agency had gathered several hundred Cuban exiles and were training them in Guatemala. The training was preparing the exiles for an invasion of Cuba and removal of Fidel Castro's communist movement (Gadney 96). President Kennedy, after listening to close advisors, approved the invasion, which is referred to as the Bay of Pigs. From the beginning, the secret invasion was disastrous because of the lack of experienced military personnel, CIA informants to Cubans, and poor planning by CIA officials. The invasion failed, and Kennedy took sole responsibility for the United States' involvement, but surprisingly, the polls showed that he gained support from the American public (Gadney 101). Kennedy, later to one of his advisors, asked, "How could I have been so far off base? All my life I've known better than to depend on the experts. How could I have been so stupid to let them go ahead?" (qtd. in Gadney 101). Kennedy realized he had made a crucial error with the Bay of Pigs invasion, and somehow escaped the wrath of the media. Reg Gadney, author of *Kennedy*, does not clearly state or understand why Kennedy did not drop in the public opinion polls but I have my suspicions. After conducting an interview with my grandfather, Walter Bragg, I became aware of the strong admiration the public had for President Kennedy. He explained how Kennedy's charm and rhetoric dumbfounded the American people. Further conversations informed me of Kennedy's capability to inspire Americans to believe that citizens and the government could combine to form a unified nation (10 Oct. 1997). As I sat and listened to my grandfather, I realized that Kennedy's youthfulness, energy, and charisma helped capture a nation that welcomed a new era of ideas and policies. A mass majority of the nation loved President Kennedy and decided that they wanted to follow him wherever he would take them. A famous quote by Kennedy states, "Ask not what your country can do for you—ask what you can do for your country" (Settel 11). His statement encouraged citizens to unify, which supports my belief that he was an effective President.

The summer of 1962 produced the emergence of Kennedy as a dominant figure in foreign affairs because of the Soviet missile buildup in Cuba. On September 13, 1962 Kennedy announced that any Soviet threat in Cuba would not be tolerated by the United States (Giglio 191). Soviet Premier Nikita Khrushchev reassured President Kennedy on many occasions that the U.S.S.R. had no desire to set up missile bases in Cuba (Abel 16). In mid October 1962, Senator Keating reported to Congress that reliable sources informed him that the Soviets had deployed troops to Cuba and were setting up missile bases (Abel 12–13). U-2 plane observations of Cuban territory confirmed Kennedy's closest advisors' suspicions that the Soviets were, in fact, setting up missile equipment in Cuba. McGeorge Bundy, President Kennedy's personal advisor, decided that it would be best to notify Kennedy on Tuesday morning, because Kennedy was fatigued and had a formal dinner party in progress (Abel 28–31). When Bundy informed him of the crisis the next morning, Kennedy immediately called for an Executive Committee meeting, which was comprised of the closest advisors to the White House (Giglio 193). The group met over a thirteen-day period until Kennedy finally received an answer to his ultimatum on 28 Oct. 1962 (Giglio 194).

Over the thirteen-day period, the Executive Committee, commonly referred to as the ExComm, met dozens of times to discuss options of Kennedy's plan of action: "Eventually they narrowed the options to two before providing the President with a recommendation that he himself preferred" (Giglio 195). These two options were either an air strike, with an invasion to follow, or a blockade. The President secretly liked the idea of a blockade and then further action if needed (Giglio 198–

99). October twenty-second marked Kennedy's address on public television to Khrushchev, which was meant to show Khrushchev that the United States would not back down to the Soviet Union (Giglio 199). Khrushchev replied to Kennedy's blockade message by sending more than twenty ships to Cuba, but at the last minute he reversed their course. Later, Khrushchev threatened to sink an American ship if Kennedy did not call off the quarantine (Giglio 207). On Saturday, 27 October, Kennedy delivered an ultimatum to Khrushchev which called for Soviet dismantlement and removal of all ground-to-air missiles and surface-to-air missiles in Cuba. Failure to comply to the United States' demands would force the President to introduce military action against the missiles in Cuba (Giglio 212). Giglio then explains how Khrushchev's response came on a beautiful fall morning. "He announced that he accepted the Kennedy proposal of the twenty-seventh, requiring the Soviets to withdraw the missiles from Cuba" (213). Khrushchev's answer ended the confrontation between the United States and the Soviet Union.

The Cuban Missile Crisis, in my opinion, helped transform a young American President into a seasoned veteran because of his tough stand against Khrushchev and the Soviet's intrusion on the Western hemisphere. Kennedy learned to be careful and precise in his decisions, considering his misfortune with the Bay of Pigs invasion. It is my belief that Kennedy evolved into a prominent world leader because of the courage and determination he demonstrated during the crisis. Many historians who write about the missile crisis repeatedly refer to Khrushchev's lack of respect for Kennedy, due to his youthfulness and ambition. I believe that Kennedy delivered an ultimatum to Khrushchev because of his frustration and anger with his lack of respect. Not recognizing the importance of Kennedy's ultimatum would be stupidity, because he sent a forceful message: do not test the United States and its willingness to insure the safety of its civilians. This moment in Kennedy's presidency, in my personal evaluation, is more significant than his assassination because of his stand against communism.

The 1960s was a time of trial and tribulation for most African-Americans in the United States. Their goals were to gain the rights that every other American was promised and already had (Lord 132–33). When Kennedy took office in 1961, the civil rights movement was already active and hostility existed (Hunt 48). Donald C. Lord, author of *John F. Kennedy*, explains:

> There were seven main areas where Kennedy could, and did, act through executive
>
> action on behalf of black America. These areas were education, transportation, pub-

lic accommodations, voting, equal justice under the law, employment, and housing.

The administration was to have some success with all but one-equal justice under

the law. (144)

Kennedy went on to create the Equal Employment Opportunity Commission, EEOC, but many civil rights leaders thought he was delaying action. In the summer of 1963, violence broke out in many Southern states and Kennedy was forced to act immediately. 19 June 1963 marks the date that Kennedy sent to congress the largest civil rights bill since the end of the Civil War (Hunt 49). Unfortunately, Kennedy did not get to see the bill passed because of his assassination, but Lyndon B. Johnson had it passed immediately after Kennedy's death (Hunt 50).

This was the largest civil rights bill passed since reconstruction and to overlook this important policy would be outrageous. Kennedy may not have been swift in enacting a civil rights policy immediately after taking the presidency in 1961, but one had to take into consideration that the Bay of Pigs, the Missile Crisis, and Vietnam had consumed much of his schedule. It's my belief that Kennedy wanted the equality of all human beings in America, and the world, and this legislation is proof. African-Americans have the right to attend any school they want, can vote without intimidation and can get jobs; Kennedy helped to better the lifestyles of African-Americans and should be praised for his courage to tackle such a controversial issue.

President Kennedy and Robert Kennedy led a dangerous fight against organized crime and corruption; the Kennedys' determination was noble, but it is believed by some that this was a major contributor to JFK's assassination. Conover Hunt, author of *JFK: For a New Generation*, discusses the possibility that the mob had JFK killed because of his efforts to shut down their operations. Hunt also explains that the Warren Commission even looked into Jack Ruby's relation to the mob (97). Jack Ruby was the lone assassin of Lee Harvey Oswald in the basement of the Dallas police department. Ruby had connections with Carlos Marcello, a mob boss in New Orleans, and Santos Trafficante, a mob boss in Florida (Hunt 96). It was later discovered that Ruby had connections with Jimmy Hoffa it is common knowledge among historians and politicians that Hoffa and Robert Kennedy hated one another (Hunt 97). It is known that during the 1960s, Hoffa was head of the Truckers Union of America and that he had close connections to the mafia. Thanks to my grandfather, Walter Bragg, I learned that it was known that the mafia wanted control over the trucking industry, so that they could, in their opinion, control America's transportation system (10 Oct. 1997). Hunt's last statement about organized crime and Kennedy was that "there have been a num ber of secretly taped conversations released in which mob leaders stated that they wanted Kennedy dead" (97). This brings me to the conclusion that maybe Kennedy's relentless stand against organized crime ultimately led to his death in Dallas. The President of the United States of America was killed in broad daylight in front of thousand of Americans on 22 November 1963, and that is in no way forgettable or excusable. Americans have the right to know what happened on that day, and to ignore the events and policies prior to the assassination would be foolish. What is important to remember is that a young, ambitious, and courageous John Kennedy inspired Americans and inhabitants all over the world with his rhetoric, intellect, and youthfulness. Considering that Kennedy was only forty-three when elected to the presidency, it is conceivable that he was beyond his years in understanding and knowledge. Policies that Kennedy proposed and enacted usually led to the improvement of Americans' way of living. Of course there were a couple of blemishes on his record, but no one is perfect. Not many presidents would want to have to address such issues as the Bay of Pigs, the Cuban missile crisis, the civil rights movement and organized crime. Overlooking his policies, in my opinion, would be a huge injustice to Kennedy and his presidency. Asking myself whether or not Kennedy left his mark on American history, I have to answer yes. His policies helped shape and form a change in America. His assassination was, and is, still important, but how long will his policies have to wait for their well deserved recognition? I believe that several of his enacted policies eventually produced his death, and it is sickening to me when a man's life is taken because a minority of people do not agree with his position on an issue.

Works Cited

Abel, Elie. *The Missile Crisis*. Philadelphia: J.B. Lippincott, 1966.

Bragg, Walter. Personal Interview. 10 Oct. 1997.

Gadney, Reg. *Kennedy*. New York: Holt and Winston, 1983.

Giglio, James N. *The Presidency of John F. Kennedy*. Kansas: U of Kansas P, 1991.

Hunt, Conover. *JFK: For a New Generation*. Arlington, TX: Authentic P, 1967.

Lord, Donald C. *John F. Kennedy: The Politics of Confrontation and Conciliation*. New York: Barron's Woodbury, 1977.

Settel, T.S. *The Wisdom of JFK*. New York: E.P. Dutton, 1965.

PAPER #5

Tiffany L. Clifton

Ms. Solis

English 104–534

20 September 2001

Gas Shortage: The Big Picture

During the past year, citizens of the United States have seen a significant rise in gas prices. In an article published in *World Oil*, Robert Snyder, explains: "Many believe recent price hikes might be the effect of alleged collusion among natural gas companies that may have agreed to cut production to drive up prices" (11). Others, however, feel that the problem lies in the growing demand for natural gas (Best 43). Politics also play an important role; A. F. Alhajji, author of "Middle East politics still dominate oil prices," claims that the "oil industry and government are so intertwined that politics is the 'main driver' in the oil market" (35). There are many forces at work in the oil industry; however, many people focus in on one issue, and fail to see the big picture.

Several analysts argue that certain factors are more accountable for the current oil and gas shortages than others. For example, they believe our former President Bill Clinton tried to help our nation by selling the strategic reserves of the United States (Tippee 24). When President Clinton released our reserves, the price of gas was drastically reduced. With the low prices, producers were not able to keep their wells producing. Numerous producers were forced out of business. After the extra gas from the strategic reserve was used, gas prices rose drastically. Hyde is quoted as saying, "Last year, when prices were lower, producers cut their production. That production cut has led to the current shortage with corresponding higher prices. By diminishing reserves of natural gas, the price is automatically driven up" (Fischer 27). When the surplus of gas hit the market, it forced the price so low that oil companies could not operate under such meager pay.

The depressed oil and gas prices in recent years have discouraged exploration of new reserves; therefore, with an increased demand for natural gas, shortages have been caused. From 1998 through 1999, the industry suffered from extremely depressed prices. In an article published in *World Oil* in 2000, Richard M. Currence summarizes the situation: "While the gas production has increased, it has not kept pace with the growth rate for oil and gas prices. Part of this stems from uncertainty over how long the higher price will last. Another reason is due to still-fresh memories of the beating that the industry took during the era of nine dollar oil as recently as two years ago"(41). Many independents are wary about the recent hike in prices; they are being cautious, because they do not know when the next crash of the oil market will occur.

"Therefore, many statisticians anticipate that the gas demand will increase more than fifty percent over the next fifteen years" (Cochener 58). "Knowing this, many forecasts of future oil and gas production depend on the drilling industry to continue increasing the annual average footages drilled per rig. This will require a strong research and investment commitment on the part of drillers and their suppliers, as well as recognition by customers that the value received from these advances justifies payment of higher rates than we have seen in the recent past" (Kelly 38). Citizens of the United States will have to be patient as the oil industry repairs all of the damage brought on, as a result of the lower prices.

There are many forces and pressures at work in the complex oil industry, and each group that is responsible for the current gas price is going to have to be willing to change their goals. The government needs to help revitalize the depleted industry so we can try to recover enough to face the growing demand for natural gas. The procedures need time to allow themselves to regain their footing. The gas shortage will not fix itself, but it will take the time and dedication of many devoted men and women to right the problem.

Works Cited

Alhajji, A.F. "Middle East politics still dictate oil prices." *World Oil*. January 2001: 35.

Best, Rhys J. "Pace picks up for service/supply firms." *World Oil*. December 2000: 43.

Cochener, John C. "US gas growth to rely heavily on Canada, Gulf of Mexico." *Oil & Gas Journal*, 22 January 2001: 58.

Currence, Richard M. "Offshore sector ready to handle challenges enroute to bright future." *World Oil*. December 2000: 41.

Fischer, Perry A. "Hyde gas prices." *World Oil*. January 2001: 27.

Kelly, Paul L. "Contract drillers see new investments in rigs begin to stir." *World Oil*. December 2000: 37, 38.

McIntyre, Douglas "Gasoline Prices: What is Happening?" Petroleum. 9 May 2001. Energy Information Administration. 13 Sept. 2001 <http://www.eia.doe.gov/oil_gas/petroleum/info_glance/petroleum.htm>.

Snyder, Robert E. "U.S. Congressman requests gas price investigation." *World Oil*. December 2000: 11.

Tippee, Bob. "Bush, Gore highlight energy strategies in debate." *Oil & Gas Journal*. 9 October 2000: 24.

Tiffany Clifton, President

Gas Shortage: The Big Picture

During the past year, we, the oil industry, have witnessed a significant rise in gas prices. Robert Snyder of World Oil points out that "many people believe recent price hikes might be the effect of alleged collusion among natural gas companies that may have agreed to cut production to drive up prices." However, that is far from the truth. With a growing demand for natural gas, the producers have run into shortages of equipment and capable, trained people. Politics are also a crucial part of this current energy crisis. According to A.F. Alhajii, we have become so entangled with the government that politics is the "main driver" in the oil market. Due to the United States government's lack of good decisions concerning the oil and gas industry, our nation will undoubtedly suffer a severe economic crisis.

Looking at our current energy crisis, I have found certain factors are more accountable for the oil and gas shortages than others. Sources published in *Oil and Gas Journal* and *World Oil* validate my claims: Our former President Bill Clinton tried to help our nation by selling the strategic reserves in 1999. When our dear President Clinton released those reserves, gas prices were drastically reduced, further crippling our industry. The lower prices made it impossible for the producers to keep their wells generating oil economically. Numerous producers were forced out of business. When the surplus of gas hit the market, it forced the price so low that even the large oil companies could not operate under such meager conditions. With the depressed oil and gas prices, the exploration of new reserves has greatly diminished; therefore, with an increased demand for natural gas, shortages have been caused. Ronald B. Gold reports that from 1998 through 1999, we have suffered from extremely depressed prices. However, Cambridge Energy Research Associates predicts that gas prices for 2001 will settle around $5.50–$6.50 per MMBtu. Richard Currence believes that "while gas production has increased, it has not kept pace with the growth rate for oil and gas prices. Another reason is due to still-fresh memories of the beating that the industry took during the era of nine dollar oil as recently as two years ago." Many of us are wary about the recent hike in prices; we are being cautious, because we do not know when the next crash will come.

John C. Cochener estimates that over the span of the next fifteen years gas demand will increase more than fifty percent. Knowing this, our nation is depending on us to keep increasing our annual footages drill per rig. "This will require a strong research and investment commitment on the part of drillers and their suppliers, "Paul Kelly from *Oil World* emphasizes. Citizens of the United States will have to be patient as we repair all to the damage brought on, as a result of lower prices.

There are many forces and pressures at work in our industry, and each of us is responsible for the current gas prices. We have to be willing to change our goals. The government needs to help us revitalize the depleted industry so we can try to recover enough to face the growing demand for natural gas. The producers need time to regain their footing. This gas shortage will not fix itself, but it will take our time and dedication to right the problem.

Clifton Exploration/ December 2001

Short List of Possible Revisions

(Consider revising an essay you have already written into one of these genres.)

- an editorial page of a newspaper or magazine
- a newsletter
- a pamphlet
- a computer slide show presentation
- a web page
- a children's book
- a manual
- a radio advertisement
- a radio broadcast
- a set of interview questions and an interview
- a television commercial
- a museum exhibit or display case
- any other medium that helps make your essay useful

Reminder:

When you are converting one type of writing to another, remember that your two most important considerations are audience and medium. You must first analyze your audience to know what they already know, what they need to know, and what medium would best convey your message to them. Make sure you choose information from your paper that is specific to your audience's needs. Edit out all information that will not be useful to the audience.

Once you know what information you wish to convey to your targeted audience, pick a medium that will best handle the information and best reach your audience. You need to consider the advantages and disadvantages of the medium you have chosen: is it print or audio/video? Are you limited by space or by time? For instance, approximately how many words will you be able to fit into a single-page pamphlet or a 5-minute interview? How will you organize your information? Where do you place the most important information in your chosen medium? How does your chosen audience's age affect your medium: do web sites for children look the same as web sites for adults?

Remember to consider audience and medium in all of your decisions about converting an academic paper into another type of document. Feel free to ask your instructor or the University Writing Center for help with the different aspects of converting one genre into another.

Part V
Writing Course Policies and Procedures

The Writing Programs Office

Director: Dr. Joanna Gibson
Associate Director: Dr. Jackie Palmer
Email: info-wpo@english.tamu.edu
Location: Blocker 224
              College Station, Texas 77843-4227
Phone: (979)845-9936
Hours: The Writing Programs Office is open Monday through Friday from 8:00 a.m. until 5:00 p.m. (The office is closed for lunch between noon and 1:00 p.m.).
Online Information: www-english.tamu.edu/wprograms

Purpose

The Writing Programs Office (WPO) administers the department's undergraduate writing courses (English 104, 203, 210, and 301), supervises GATs and lecturers teaching these courses, oversees the department's computer classrooms, and coordinates a grading program for the English 104 proficiency exam. We are responsible for the quality of teaching in these courses and student access to them. In addition, we handle all matters pertaining to the courses (e.g., textbook selection, plagiarism, and behavioral cases).

Our goals are twofold:

- to ensure the quality of undergraduate writing courses and
- to prepare departmental graduate students for professions as writers, teachers, and editors.

For undergraduate English 104, 203, 210, and 301 students, we offer:

- Information (print and electronic) about writing courses, placing out of English 104, and course substitutions
- Forcing for international and technical writing sections
- Grade appeals
- Mediation services
- Course syllabi
- Electronic resources to supplement writing courses
- Advising for the Professional Writing Certificate and the Society for Technical Communication

Because writing courses require student participation and teacher evaluation, we do not permit audits.

Policies

Auditing of Writing Courses

Writing instructors may not allow auditing of their courses. Instruction in writing requires active participation in class and frequent feedback from the instructor in the form of written and oral comments. Writing classes are capped at 25–28 students (depending on the course and the semester) to ensure that students receive as much individual attention as possible. Therefore, auditing is not feasible and is not permitted.

Attending the Section You Are Enrolled In

It is your responsibility to attend the section in which you are officially enrolled. If, for some reason, you attend a section in which you are not enrolled, you will be required to switch to the section in which you are enrolled. Neither purchase of textbooks not completion of assignments is a valid reason for attending a section in which you are not enrolled. The Writing Programs Office will not make exceptions. To avoid confusion, check your fee slip carefully, noting days of the week, time of day, and room numbers.

Classroom Behavior

In general, classroom behavior is not a problem for students who use good sense and good manners. These reminders are offered, however, so that you will understand how the Writing Programs Office and the University will deal with behavior/attitude problems.

University Rules address acceptable and unacceptable classroom behavior (see policy on Disruptive Activity, TAMU Student Rule 21, Revised: 1995). Any of the following may constitute behavior that seriously interferes with your instructor's ability to conduct class or the ability of other students to profit from instruction:

- sleeping, reading anything other than in-class reading assignments, writing anything other than inclass writing assignments;
- leaving class early without permission from the instructor;
- being habitually late to class; and
- talking to other students when the instructor is talking or when another student is asking a question or making a presentation.

In addition, your instructor may object to your bringing food or beverages to class. Many classrooms have signs posted that prohibit food or drinks in the room. You should observe these guidelines.

Students who exhibit aggressive or rude behavior —either in class or in an instructor's office—will also be subjected to disciplinary action as outlined in the Student Rules. Incidents reported to the Student Conflict Resolution Center, Office of Students Affairs, are also reported to a student's dean.

Incompletes

TAMU Student Rules outline situations in which a grade of incomplete (*I*) is appropriate. Incompletes can only be given with the permission of your instructor, who must consult with the Writing Programs Director before making a decision about giving you an incomplete. The Writing Programs Director will consider requests for a grade of *I* only if you have completed 50 percent of the coursework. In addition, you may be required to submit a form from your college advising office. Even if 50 percent of the work is completed, an incomplete will be refused unless the conditions specified in *TAMU Student Rules, Section 10.5 (Revised 2001)*, are met.

These regulations state that an incomplete be given only when absences have been authorized or when the cause for the incomplete work is beyond the student's control.

If you must take an incomplete, document your reasons as completely as possible.

If circumstances take you away from class, see your instructor and academic advisor as soon as possible to keep them informed. The longer you are AWOL without explanation, the harder it will be to prove that you are doing everything in your power to complete your course.

Attendance

According to TAMU Student Rule 7, with the exception of illness or injury where the student has been treated by the Health Center, the student is responsible for providing evidence to the instructor of the reason for any absence. The Student Rules further state that "if no evidence is available, the instructor will decide whether the absence is to be excused" (TAMU Student Rules, Section 7).

Illness

If you have not been treated by a doctor, your absence from class may or may not be excused. Your instructor will decide. You should notify your instructor before you miss a class by leaving a message on the department answering machine at 845–3454. Be sure to identify yourself clearly (first name and last name, instructor's name, and section number). By calling this number and leaving a message, you do not have to play phone tag with your instructor, and you can be sure your message will be received.

If you have been treated by a doctor, you should provide your instructor with a note or letter from the doctor, stating when you were treated and listing any dates when you should be excused from classes. The Health Center uses a standard form. This type of documentation is required if you are requesting an excused absence.

Prescriptions are not considered adequate documentation of illness.

Other Reasons for Missing Classes

University Rules specify reasons deemed sufficient for missing class and provide outlines and guidelines for the length of time students have to make up assignments. You are responsible for documenting (that is, providing information in writing) any reason for missing class.

If illness or death in your immediate family affects attendance in all of your classes, you should see an advisor in your college advising office. Advisors can help you document the situation and verify that you are having a legitimate problem.

Check your instructor's attendance policy. Ask for clarification if you are not entirely clear on the policy. Make sure you understand all penalties for unexcused absences.

If you miss a class because of an excused absence, your instructor is obliged to allow you to make up homework, class work or exams. But you are responsible for following TAMU Student Rules and initiating arrangements for making up work. An excused absence is not a license to avoid required work. Check Student Rules for the time frame for submitting missed assignments. (TAMU Student Rules, Section 7.5, Revised 1999.)

Plagiarism

Plagiarism is the unauthorized and unacknowledged use of the ideas or words of another person. For a better understanding of what constitutes plagiarism, see section III ("Recognizing Plagiarism") of this book.

If your instructor finds evidence that you have plagiarized, he or she will provide you with an opportunity to explain the situation. If your instructor concludes that plagiarism has occurred, he or she will write a letter to the Head of the English Department recommending a sanction. A copy of this letter will be given to you. The Department Head will review the evidence and make a ruling. The Department Head may uphold, dismiss, reduce, or increase the recommended sanction.

The Writing Programs Office considers plagiarism a serious problem. Should a student submit a plagiarized paper, the Writing Programs Office urges instructors to impose a sanction of F in the course and to place a letter of reprimand in the student's file. This letter can be accessed only by an authorized administrator and would be accessed if another disciplinary problem arises. It does not appear on a SIMS screen or on the official TAMU transcript.

A student may appeal sanctions to the Head of the English Department within five days after notification of charges. If that appeal is unsuccessful, the student may appeal to the Dean of Liberal Arts. The process is outlined in *TAMU Student Rules* (Section 20, revised 1999).

Late Assignments

All assignments must be submitted on time. Your instructor will have a policy about late assignments on your class syllabus. Be sure you understand that policy. A late paper can receive a substantial penalty.

If you miss a deadline because of an excused absence, you should get the assignment to the instructor as soon as possible. Contact the instructor to let him or her know what is happening and to arrange to turn in your work late.

You must complete all assigned work to receive a grade other than *F* in the course, even if your average grade is passing without all the work completed.

Picking Up Assignments and Posted Grades

According to the Family Education Rights and Privacy Act of 1974 (see *TAMU Student Rules*, Appendix III), your instructor may not release grade information. For security reasons, your instructor will not give out grades over the phone—to you, your parents, other instructors, and University administrators. One exception is certain department administrators (such as the Director of Writing Programs).

Your instructor will not post grades, even by pseudonyms or Social Security numbers, unless you have given written permission (*TAMU Student Rules*, section 10.16, revised 2001).

Your instructor may suggest that you provide a self-addressed, stamped postcard or envelope so that your final grades may be mailed to you.

To pick up end-of-semester assignments: Either pick up work during office hours, arrange to have the

paper mailed to you (but provide a self-addressed, manila envelope with enough postage), or stop by during the instructor's office hours during the next semester. If the instructor is away for that semester, or has left TAMU, check with the Writing Programs secretary. She may be able to locate the instructor or the work.

Completed assignments are kept for approximately one semester after the course has ended. After that, any assignments that have not been picked up are recycled—that is, the paper is recycled, not your work.

Grade Appeals for English 104

POLICY STATEMENT

According to *TAMU Student Rules*, a student may appeal *a final course grade* that he or she believes is "capricious, arbitrary or prejudiced" (Section 48, revised 1995). Only the involved student may initiate a formal appeal (see *TAMU Student Rules*, "Family Educational Rights and Privacy Act of 1974", Appendix III). Procedures for initiating a formal grade appeal are outlined below.

> According to TAMU regulations, any grade appeal must begin with the student's instructor. If no satisfactory resolution is reached with the instructor, or if the instructor is unavailable, the student will submit the grade appeal to the Writing Programs Office.

The Writing Programs Office will forward the appeal to the Department Head for review. To be considered for a review, a grade appeal must be presented according to the following guidelines. If a grade is appealed, the student's grade on any contested assignments (and therefore the final grade) may be either raised or lowered according to recommendations made during the review process.

At the request of the Department Head, a committee of three faculty members appointed by the Director of Writing Programs will review grade appeals and inform the Department Head in writing whether or not they find an instructor's final course evaluation to be capricious, arbitrary, or prejudiced. After considering the student's appeal and the review committee's recommendations, the Department Head will rule on the grade appeal.

WHEN APPEALS WILL BE ACCEPTED

Appeals must be initiated in writing with the course instructor, or if the course instructor is unavailable, with the Writing Programs Office, within 180 days (six months) of the last day of the semester or summer session in which the disputed grade was earned.

While students have 180 days for a grade appeal, the Writing Programs Office requests that, in order to expedite the appeal process, the students submit appeals by the Wednesday of the third week of the term after the course in question is completed.

WHICH ASSIGNMENTS MAY BE APPEALED

Students who believe that one or more assignments reflect capricious, arbitrary, or prejudiced evaluation may ask that these assignments be reviewed. **It is the student's responsibility to establish a *prima facie*** case of capricious, arbitrary, or prejudiced academic evaluation.

All assignments completed by the student during the semester must be submitted along with the assignments in question. The assignments in question must be clearly identified.

PROCEDURES FOR SUBMITTING APPEALS

Students must place in a manila folder the following items:

Letter to the Department Head. In this letter, the student will explain specifically why he or she believes a case of capricious, arbitrary, or prejudiced academic evaluation exists, and specify the assignment in question.

The student should also include a mailing address and phone number at which he or she can be reached.

The syllabus for the course. This is the syllabus the instructor gave each class member at the first class meeting.

All assignments. If the student does not have copies of the assignments, the Writing Programs secretary will contact the instructor and request that the student's file be given to the Writing Programs Office and then to the Department Head.

The student will leave the completed folder with the Writing Programs Office.

The Department Head will see that each petition is reviewed. If the Department Head or Director of Writing Programs needs additional information or wishes to meet with the student, the student will be notified by phone or by written request. The student will be contacted in writing as to the decision reached.

The process for appealing the Department Head's decision is outlined in *TAMU Student Rules*, Section 48.

Support Services for Students with Disabilities

Services for Students with Disabilities (a branch of the Department of Student Life) aims to offer a "barrier free" environment for Aggies, as they state in their brochure, an environment free from both physical and attitudinal barriers.

They provide a number of services, personalized to meet each client's needs, to help students succeed at TAMU. For example, their services include notification to professors, requests for extra time for test-taking, reduced distraction environments for test taking, assistance with registration, sign language interpreters and much more. They also help TAMU students with access to campus facilities. And they serve as an advocacy group, educating professors, students, staff, and administrators on campus about issues related to students with disabilities.

To be eligible for these services, you must be able to document your disability, and you must register with their office at the beginning of each semester. For more information, contact Services for Students with Disabilities at 845–1637. Or visit the website at: http://ats.tamu.edu/

Grade Descriptions

Your instructor may provide a description of letter grades more specific to your section, but if not, this general description will give you an accurate picture of how papers are evaluated.

A paper: The A paper is a pleasure to read. It is fully developed, leaving the reader with no unanswered questions or unsatisfied objections. It considers the reader's needs—questions, possible objections, basic information—and fulfills them. All research material is properly documented and gracefully worked into the text as support for the author's claims or ideas. In addition, the information and/or arguments are logically ordered to meet the reader's needs. The A paper is marked by stylistic finesse: the title and opening paragraph are engaging; transitions are artful; phrasing is tight, fresh, and highly specific; sentence structure is varied; tone enhances the purpose of the paper. Finally, the A paper, because of its careful organization and development, imparts a feeling of wholeness and unusual clarity. Not surprisingly, then, it leaves the reader feeling bright, thoroughly satisfied, and eager to reread the piece.

B paper: It is significantly more than competent. Besides being almost free of mechanical errors, the B paper delivers substantial information and makes cogent, fresh arguments—that is, in both quality and interest-value. Its specific points are logically ordered, well-developed and supported, and unified around a clear organizing principle that is apparent early in the paper. The opening paragraph draws the reader in; the closing paragraphs are for the most part smooth, the sentence structure pleasingly varied. The diction of the B paper is typically much more concise and precise than that found in the C paper. At times it shows distinctiveness—that is, finesse and memorableness. On the whole, then, a B paper makes the reading experience a pleasurable one, for it offers substantial information or argument with few distractions, and it takes into account the needs of its readers.

C paper: It is generally competent; it meets the assignment, has few mechanical errors (and these do not seriously interfere with readability), and is reasonably well-organized and developed. The actual information it delivers, however, seems thin and commonplace and its arguments are ordinary and worn. One reason for that impression is that the ideas are typically cast in the form of vague and under developed generalities—generalities that ignore the reader's needs, prompting him or her to ask: "In every case?" "Exactly how large?" "Why" "But how many?" Stylistically the C paper has other shortcomings as well: the opening paragraph does little to draw the reader in; the final paragraph offers only a perfunctory "wrap-up"; transitions between paragraphs are often bumpy; sentences, besides being a bit choppy, tend to follow a predictable (hence monotonous) subjectverb- object pattern and a sing-songy rhythm; and diction is occasionally marred by unconscious repetitions, redundancy, and imprecision. Documentation is correct and quotes are properly, if not always gracefully, incorporated into the prose. The C paper, then, while it gets the job done, lacks both imagination and intellectual rigor, and hence does not invite rereading.

D paper: Its treatment and development of the subject are as yet only rudimentary. While organization is present, it is neither clear nor effective.

The thesis may be unclear or difficult to find, and claims not well-supported. Sentences are frequently awkward, ambiguous, and marred by serious mechanical errors. Evidence of careful proofreading is scanty, if nonexistent. There is little sense of an actual reader with expectations and needs to be fulfilled. Documentation may be poorly done, and quoting and paraphrasing are awkward.

F paper: Its treatment of the subject is superficial; its theme lacks discernible organization; its prose is confusing and stylistically inadequate. Mechanical errors are frequent. In short, the ideas, organization, and style fall far below what is acceptable for college writing. An *F* paper might also be one that does not fulfill the assignment or that is plagiarized.

Computing and
Information Service Labs

Computing and Information Services (CIS) maintains numerous open-access computing facilities all over campus. (Open-access means the labs are open to TAMU students, staff, and faculty.) You will find these labs indispensable for many writing tasks, as they supply word processing, document design, spreadsheet, and graphics programs for IBM and Macintosh microcomputers. They also provide access to email, the Internet (the World Wide Web, for example), printers, and scanners. Finally, consultants at the CIS help desks can assist you with various computer problems, including getting an email address, setting up your home computer, or scanning graphics into your text.

CIS Lab/Help Desk Directory

For a useful map of the computing facilities on campus, consult the booklet "*Computing at Texas A&M: A World of Opportunity*", available around campus, especially at the sites listed below. Or check out the CIS home page (http://www.tamu.edu/scip). There is a link to the campus map which shows lab locations.

CIS Labs are located in the following buildings:

Biochemistry & Biophysics	106 BICH
Blocker	133D BLOC
Read	150 READ
Network Availability Center	112 OETW
Teague Graphics Lab	1002 TEAG
West Campus Library	137 WCL
Wisenbaker Engineering Research Center	024 WERC

Help Desk Central (845–8300; HELPDESK@TAMU.EDU; http://www.tamu.edu/scip) can also answer questions about the CIS labs. This is the place to call if you cannot get help from the desk in the lab where you are working, or if your are working from home.

- Be patient. If there is a long line at the help desk, try calling or emailing Help Desk Central.
- All Help Desk staff cannot answer every question you might have, and they often have to solve problems as best they can—sometimes without explaining every step to you.
- Bear in mind that you have paid not only for access to computing facilities but also for help. If you feel you have not been adequately helped, send email to (or call) Help Desk Central and give as many details about the situation as you can. If you still need help, send email to Dr. John Rauser john-rauser@tamu.edu.
- Check out the CIS documentation, available on a variety of topics. Documentation can be picked up from computer labs around campus. You can also call 845–8300 for help in getting some documentation via your computer, or use the World Wide Web: (http://www.tamu.edu/scip).

Release for Use of Student Writing

The writing that I produced in English_____ Section_____ during the Spring, Summer or Fall, _____, may be reproduced by the English Department, Texas A&M University.

I understand that my papers may also be used in writing courses or other publications, such as *Writing Tradi-tions*, as an example of exemplary student writing, or in publications addressed to scholarly readers to promote research in the teaching of writing. If my writing is chosen for publication of this sort, I will be contacted to give explicit permission. This form will be used to help authors contact me.

Name (please print) _____

Name (signature) _____

Student ID number _____

Permanent address _____

City/State/Zip Code _____

Permanent telephone number _____

Local address _____

Local telephone number _____

Date _____

Professional Writing Certificate

The Professional Writing Certificate is awarded by the TAMU English Department's Writing Programs office. It recognizes 18 hours of intensive training in a broad range of communication skills. You should allow at least a year and a half to complete the schedule of courses, some of which are offered only once a year.

Eligibility

You are eligible to participate if:

- You are a Texas A&M undergraduate.
- You are an English major who thus cannot receive a minor in English, or you are a major in any other area that does not allow a minor.

Other limitations:

- You may **not** participate in the certification program if you complete the minor in English with an Emphasis in Professional Writing.
- You may **not** substitute transfer courses, independent studies, or credit by exam for any of the required courses.*
- You must complete all coursework by the semester you graduate. If this is not possible, you may petition the Writing Committee for an extension.
- **You must earn a grade of B or better** in all courses.

Required Courses

You must complete the following 12 hours of coursework, earning a grade of B or better in each class:

English 210	*Scientific and Technical Writing*—covers the principles of rhetoric and communication applied to the analysis and composition of the main genres of scientific and technical writing, including the report, proposal, and manual. (***Note:** Students with AP credit for ENGL 210 must take 301.)
or	
English 301	*Technical Writing*—explores advanced writing in technical, scientific, and business fields: memos, letters, proposals and various types of business and industry reports.
English 241	*Advanced Composition*—focuses on pattern and style in effective prose through analysis and writing of expository, descriptive and argumentative essays of length and sophistication. (*Note: Students with AP credit for ENGL 241 must substitute an additional course from the list of electives.)
English 320	*Technical Editing*—covers designing, editing, and publishing technical documents.
English 355	*Rhetoric of Style*—explores and develops style through analysis, historical study, and practice.

Electives
In addition to the four required courses (12 hours), student must select two courses (6 hours) from the following list:

ENGL 353 *History of Modern Rhetoric*	JOUR 203 *Media Writing*	SCOM 203 *Public Speaking*
ENGL 354 *Modern Rhetorical Theory*	JOUR 210 *Graphics*	SCOM 301 *Rhetoric in Western Thought*
ENGL 489 *Special Topics in Technical Communication* (can be repeated, if topics differ)	JOUR 303 *Media Writing II*	SCOM 305 *Speech Communication*
	JOUR 309 *Magazine Editing and Production*	SCOM 320 *Organizational Communication*

Listserv
As a candidate for the Professional Writing Certificate, you may subscribe to the PWC listserv. This monitored forum is for notification purposes, rather than discussion; you may, however, post messages that will be screened by the listserv moderator. All job announcements (including co-ops and internships) received by the Writing Programs Office are forwarded across this list.

To subscribe, send e-mail to listserv@listserv.tamu.edu. In the body of the message type: SUBSCRIBE pwc-list firstname lastname

Certificate
Upon completing all of the coursework for the WC, you must provide the Writing Programs Office with a copy of your transcript; this will serve as evidence of completion, and as a record of the grades you have earned. If necessary, for any course completed during your final semester, you may submit a letter from your professor certifying completion of the course and the grade received. (This will avoid the necessity of submitting a complete transcript after you have left the University.)

Questions and Problems
If you have any difficulties signing up for the necessary courses or any questions about the program, you can reach the PWC advisor at wpo-grad@tamu.edu or 862-3038.